THE STADIUM EVENTS SPORTS CARD CHECKLIST

- VINTAGE FOOTBALL EDITION

TODD HUTSON

Order this book online at www.trafford.com
or email orders@trafford.com

Most Trafford titles are also available at major online book retailers.

Chris Demoff : Technical Assistance.
My Family: Loving & Supporting me.
My MOM: I LOVE you and miss you MOM!!!

Print information available on the last page.

ISBN: 978-1-4251-6791-2 (sc)

Trafford rev. 02/23/2019

www.trafford.com

North America & international
toll-free: 1 888 232 4444 (USA & Canada)
fax: 812 355 4082

INTRODUCTION

The Stadium Events Sports Card Checklist is designed to make card collecting easy. The Spiral binder allows you to flip to a particular set, and creates a flat surface for writing. The larger primary sets have their own page, whereas the smaller subsets are shared with 2 or 3 per page. Quite a few of the sets have sample cards for quick identification. Some of the sets are unnumbered so you will only see blank squares – the names can be written next to the square for identification. There are additional blank squares on each page to inventory cards that do not have numbers (Checklists, etc), and blank pages spaced throughout the book for additional notes. The Stadium Events Sports Card Checklist allows for easy access and editing of cards you need and cards you have. It is a great tool to use while you are attending Card Shows and visiting Card Stores.

Quick and easy access to the cards you are searching for, and the cards you already have!!!

<u>Tips for use:</u>

- ✓ **, X, or shade in the box**, preferably with pencil as inventories can change.
- **2** You can also write the number of cards you have in each square. This is a great way to keep track if you are trading or selling cards and only want to do this with cards you have multiples of.

Table Of Contents

TABLE OF CONTENTS

TABLE OF CONTENTS

Table Of Contents

Table Of Contents

THE ORIGINALS

1888 N-162 BEECHER (COLLEGE)

☐ ☐ ☐

KEY CARDS I HAVE: ____________________

KEY CARDS I NEED: ____________________

COMMENTS: ____________________

1 Card Set

OF CARDS I HAVE: ________

OF CARDS I NEED: ________

% OF SET FILLED: ________

1894 MAYO (COLLEGE)

KEY CARDS I HAVE: ____________________

KEY CARDS I NEED: ____________________

COMMENTS: ____________________

35 Card Set

OF CARDS I HAVE: ________

OF CARDS I NEED: ________

% OF SET FILLED: ________

1907 MICHIGAN POSTCARDS (COLLEGE)

1 ☐	5 ☐	9 ☐	13 ☐
2 ☐	6 ☐	10 ☐	14 ☐
3 ☐	7 ☐	11 ☐	15 ☐
4 ☐	8 ☐	12 ☐	

KEY CARDS I HAVE: ____________________

KEY CARDS I NEED: ____________________

COMMENTS: ____________________

15 Card Set

OF CARDS I HAVE: ________

OF CARDS I NEED: ________

% OF SET FILLED: ________

1926 SHOTWELLS

1 2 3 4 5 6 7 8 9 10 11 12 13 14 15 16 17 18 19 20 21 22 23 24

KEY CARDS I HAVE:

KEY CARDS I NEED:

COMMENTS:

OF CARDS I HAVE:

OF CARDS I NEED:

% OF SET FILLED:

24 Card Set

1926 SPALDING SPORTS CO. OF AMERICA (NFL)

1 2 3 4 5 6 7 8 9 10 11 12 13 14 15

KEY CARDS I HAVE:

KEY CARDS I NEED:

COMMENTS:

CHAMPIONS

INTERNATIONAL PHOTO

"RED" GRANGE
FOOTBALL

OF CARDS I HAVE:

OF CARDS I NEED:

% OF SET FILLED:

15 Card Set

1929 PEOPLE'S BAKING

1 2 3 4

KEY CARDS I HAVE:

KEY CARDS I NEED:

COMMENTS:

OF CARDS I HAVE:

OF CARDS I NEED:

% OF SET FILLED:

4 Card Set

1930 NOTRE DAME POSTCARDS (COLLEGE)

1 ☐
2 ☐
3 ☐
4 ☐
5 ☐
6 ☐
7 ☐
8 ☐
9 ☐
10 ☐
11 ☐
12 ☐
13 ☐
14 ☐
15 ☐
16 ☐
17 ☐
18 ☐
19 ☐
20 ☐
21 ☐
22 ☐
23 ☐
24 ☐
25 ☐

OF CARDS I HAVE:

OF CARDS I NEED:

% OF SET FILLED:

KEY CARDS I HAVE:

KEY CARDS I NEED:

COMMENTS:

1933 DIAMOND MATCHBOOKS SILVER (NFL)

OF CARDS I HAVE:

OF CARDS I NEED:

% OF SET FILLED:

KEY CARDS I HAVE:

KEY CARDS I NEED:

COMMENTS:

1934 DIAMOND MATCHBOOKS

1934 DIAMOND MATCHBOOKS (NFL)

OF CARDS I HAVE:

OF CARDS I NEED:

% OF SET FILLED:

KEY CARDS I HAVE:

KEY CARDS I NEED:

COMMENTS:

121 Card Set

1934 DIAMOND MATCHBOOKS COLLEGE RIVALS (COLLEGE)

OF CARDS I HAVE:

KEY CARDS I HAVE:

KEY CARDS I NEED:

OF CARDS I NEED:

COMMENTS:

% OF SET FILLED:

12 Card Set

1934

1934 SPORTS KINGS

1 ☐	8 ☐	15 ☐	22 ☐	29 ☐	☐
2 ☐	9 ☐	16 ☐	23 ☐	30 ☐	☐
3 ☐	10 ☐	17 ☐	24 ☐	31 ☐	☐
4 ☐	11 ☐	18 ☐	25 ☐	32 ☐	☐
5 ☐	12 ☐	19 ☐	26 ☐	33 ☐	☐
6 ☐	13 ☐	20 ☐	27 ☐	34 ☐	☐
7 ☐	14 ☐	21 ☐	28 ☐	35 ☐	☐

OF CARDS I HAVE: ______

OF CARDS I NEED: ______

% OF SET FILLED: ______

KEY CARDS I HAVE: ______

KEY CARDS I NEED: ______

COMMENTS: ______

35 Card Set

1934 SPORTS KINGS GAME CARDS

1 ☐	6 ☐	11 ☐	16 ☐	21 ☐
2 ☐	7 ☐	12 ☐	17 ☐	22 ☐
3 ☐	8 ☐	13 ☐	18 ☐	23 ☐
4 ☐	9 ☐	14 ☐	19 ☐	☐
5 ☐	10 ☐	15 ☐	20 ☐	☐

SPORT KINGS
Varsity
FOOTBALL GAME
by the makers of
SPORT KINGS GUM
THE GOUDEY GUM CO.
BOSTON, MASS.
U.S.A.

OF CARDS I HAVE: ______

OF CARDS I NEED: ______

% OF SET FILLED: ______

KEY CARDS I HAVE: ______

KEY CARDS I NEED: ______

COMMENTS: ______

23 Card Set

1934 YALO

1 ☐ 2 ☐ ☐ ☐ ☐

OF CARDS I HAVE: ______

OF CARDS I NEED: ______

% OF SET FILLED: ______

KEY CARDS I HAVE: ______

KEY CARDS I NEED: ______

COMMENTS: ______

2 Card Set

1935 DIAMOND MATCHBOOKS

1935 DIAMOND MATCHBOOKS (NFL)

KEY CARDS I HAVE:

OF CARDS I HAVE:

KEY CARDS I NEED:

OF CARDS I NEED:

COMMENTS:

% OF SET FILLED:

96 Card Set

1935 DIAMOND MATCHBOOKS COLLEGE RIVALS (COLLEGE)

KEY CARDS I HAVE:

OF CARDS I HAVE:

KEY CARDS I NEED:

OF CARDS I NEED:

COMMENTS:

% OF SET FILLED:

12 Card Set

1935

1935 NATIONAL CHICLE (NFL)

1 ☐	11 ☐	21 ☐	31 ☐
2 ☐	12 ☐	22 ☐	32 ☐
3 ☐	13 ☐	23 ☐	33 ☐
4 ☐	14 ☐	24 ☐	34 ☐
5 ☐	15 ☐	25 ☐	35 ☐
6 ☐	16 ☐	26 ☐	36 ☐
7 ☐	17 ☐	27 ☐	☐
8 ☐	18 ☐	28 ☐	☐
9 ☐	19 ☐	29 ☐	☐
10 ☐	20 ☐	30 ☐	☐

KEY CARDS I HAVE: ______

KEY CARDS I NEED: ______

COMMENTS: ______

OF CARDS I HAVE: ______

OF CARDS I NEED: ______

% OF SET FILLED: ______

36 Card Set

1935 R311-2 PREMIUM PHOTOS (NFL / COLLEGE)

KEY CARDS I HAVE: ______

KEY CARDS I NEED: ______

COMMENTS: ______

OF CARDS I HAVE: ______

OF CARDS I NEED: ______

% OF SET FILLED: ______

17 Card Set

1935 Wheaties

1935 Wheaties All Americans (College)

1☐ 4☐ 7☐ 10☐ ☐
2☐ 5☐ 8☐ 11☐ ☐
3☐ 6☐ 9☐ 12☐ ☐

Key cards I have: ______________________

____

Key cards I need: ______________________

____

Comments: ______________________

____

12 Card Set

# of cards I have: ______

# of cards I need: ______

% of set filled: ______

1935 Wheaties Fancy Frames (College)

1☐ 3☐ 5☐ 7☐ ☐
2☐ 4☐ 6☐ 8☐ ☐

Key cards I have: ______________________

____

Key cards I need: ______________________

____

Comments: ______________________

____

____

8 Card Set

# of cards I have: ______

# of cards I need: ______

% of set filled: ______

1936 DIAMOND MATCHBOOKS (NFL)

KEY CARDS I HAVE:

OF CARDS I HAVE:

OF CARDS I NEED:

% OF SET FILLED:

KEY CARDS I NEED:

COMMENTS:

1936 WHEATIES

1936 WHEATIES ALL AMERICANS (COLLEGE)

1 ☐ 5 ☐ 9 ☐ ☐
2 ☐ 6 ☐ 10 ☐ ☐
3 ☐ 7 ☐ 11 ☐ ☐
4 ☐ 8 ☐ 12 ☐ ☐

OF CARDS I HAVE: ________

OF CARDS I NEED: ________

% OF SET FILLED: ________

KEY CARDS I HAVE:

KEY CARDS I NEED:

COMMENTS:

12 Card Set

1936 WHEATIES COACHES (COLLEGE)

1 ☐ 3 ☐ 5 ☐ 7 ☐ ☐
2 ☐ 4 ☐ 6 ☐ ☐ ☐

OF CARDS I HAVE: ________

OF CARDS I NEED: ________

% OF SET FILLED: ________

KEY CARDS I HAVE:

KEY CARDS I NEED:

COMMENTS:

7 Card Set

1936 WHEATIES SIX MAN (COLLEGE)

1 ☐ 3 ☐ 5 ☐ ☐
2 ☐ 4 ☐ 6 ☐ ☐

OF CARDS I HAVE: ________

OF CARDS I NEED: ________

% OF SET FILLED: ________

KEY CARDS I HAVE:

KEY CARDS I NEED:

COMMENTS:

6 Card Set

1937

1937 DIAMOND MATCHBOOKS (NFL)

KEY CARDS I HAVE:

KEY CARDS I NEED:

COMMENTS:

OF CARDS I HAVE:

OF CARDS I NEED:

% OF SET FILLED:

24 Card Set

1937 KELLOGG'S SPORTS STAMPS

1 ☐ 2 ☐ ☐ ☐

KEY CARDS I HAVE:

KEY CARDS I NEED:

COMMENTS:

OF CARDS I HAVE:

OF CARDS I NEED:

% OF SET FILLED:

2 Card Set

1937 CONT.

1937 MAYFAIR CANDIES (NFL)

1 ☐	6 ☐	11 ☐	16 ☐	21 ☐
2 ☐	7 ☐	12 ☐	17 ☐	22 ☐
3 ☐	8 ☐	13 ☐	18 ☐	23 ☐
4 ☐	9 ☐	14 ☐	19 ☐	24 ☐
5 ☐	10 ☐	15 ☐	20 ☐	☐

KEY CARDS I HAVE: ____________________

____

KEY CARDS I NEED: ____________________

____

COMMENTS: ____________________

____

OF CARDS I HAVE: ____________

OF CARDS I NEED: ____________

% OF SET FILLED: ____________

24 Card Set

1937 WHEATIES BIG TEN (COLLEGE)

1 ☐ 2 ☐ 3 ☐ 4 ☐ 5 ☐ ☐

KEY CARDS I HAVE: ____________________

____

KEY CARDS I NEED: ____________________

____

COMMENTS: ____________________

____

OF CARDS I HAVE: ____________

OF CARDS I NEED: ____________

% OF SET FILLED: ____________

5 Card Set

1938 Diamond Matchbooks (NFL)

of cards I have:

Key cards I have:

# of cards I need:

% of set filled:

Key cards I need:

Comments:

1939

1939 GRIDIRON GREATS BLOTTERS (COLLEGE)

3941 ☐
3942 ☐
3943 ☐
3944 ☐
3945 ☐
3946 ☐
3947 ☐
3948 ☐
3949 ☐
3950 ☐
3951 ☐
3952 ☐

KEY CARDS I HAVE:

KEY CARDS I NEED:

COMMENTS:

OF CARDS I HAVE:

OF CARDS I NEED:

% OF SET FILLED:

12 Card Set

1939 REDSKINS MATCHBOOKS (NFL)

KEY CARDS I HAVE:

KEY CARDS I NEED:

COMMENTS:

OF CARDS I HAVE:

OF CARDS I NEED:

% OF SET FILLED:

20 Card Set

1940'S REDSKINS MATCHBOOKS

1940 REDSKINS MATCHBOOKS (NFL)

\# OF CARDS I HAVE:

\# OF CARDS I NEED:

% OF SET FILLED:

KEY CARDS I HAVE:

KEY CARDS I NEED:

COMMENTS:

20 Card Set

1941 REDSKINS MATCHBOOKS (NFL)

\# OF CARDS I HAVE:

\# OF CARDS I NEED:

% OF SET FILLED:

KEY CARDS I HAVE:

KEY CARDS I NEED:

COMMENTS:

20 Card Set

1942 REDSKINS MATCHBOOKS (NFL)

\# OF CARDS I HAVE:

\# OF CARDS I NEED:

% OF SET FILLED:

KEY CARDS I HAVE:

KEY CARDS I NEED:

COMMENTS:

20 Card Set

1946 AND 1948 - 52

1946 BROWNS SEARS (NFL)

1 3 5 7
2 4 6 8

KEY CARDS I HAVE:

KEY CARDS I NEED:

COMMENTS:

OF CARDS I HAVE:

OF CARDS I NEED:

% OF SET FILLED:

8 Card Set

1948 - 52 EXHIBIT W468 (NFL)

KEY CARDS I HAVE:

KEY CARDS I NEED:

COMMENTS:

OF CARDS I HAVE:

OF CARDS I NEED:

% OF SET FILLED:

59 Card Set

1948 BOWMAN (NFL)

1 ☐	16 ☐	31 ☐	46 ☐	61 ☐	76 ☐	91 ☐	106 ☐
2 ☐	17 ☐	32 ☐	47 ☐	62 ☐	77 ☐	92 ☐	107 ☐
3 ☐	18 ☐	33 ☐	48 ☐	63 ☐	78 ☐	93 ☐	108 ☐
4 ☐	19 ☐	34 ☐	49 ☐	64 ☐	79 ☐	94 ☐	☐
5 ☐	20 ☐	35 ☐	50 ☐	65 ☐	80 ☐	95 ☐	☐
6 ☐	21 ☐	36 ☐	51 ☐	66 ☐	81 ☐	96 ☐	☐
7 ☐	22 ☐	37 ☐	52 ☐	67 ☐	82 ☐	97 ☐	☐
8 ☐	23 ☐	38 ☐	53 ☐	68 ☐	83 ☐	98 ☐	☐
9 ☐	24 ☐	39 ☐	54 ☐	69 ☐	84 ☐	99 ☐	☐
10 ☐	25 ☐	40 ☐	55 ☐	70 ☐	85 ☐	100 ☐	☐
11 ☐	26 ☐	41 ☐	56 ☐	71 ☐	86 ☐	101 ☐	☐
12 ☐	27 ☐	42 ☐	57 ☐	72 ☐	87 ☐	102 ☐	☐
13 ☐	28 ☐	43 ☐	58 ☐	73 ☐	88 ☐	103 ☐	☐
14 ☐	29 ☐	44 ☐	59 ☐	74 ☐	89 ☐	104 ☐	☐
15 ☐	30 ☐	45 ☐	60 ☐	75 ☐	90 ☐	105 ☐	☐

OF CARDS I HAVE: ____________

OF CARDS I NEED: ____________

% OF SET FILLED: ____________

KEY CARDS I HAVE: ____________

KEY CARDS I NEED: ____________

COMMENTS: ____________

1948 LEAF (NFL)

1 ☐	16 ☐	31 ☐	46 ☐	61 ☐	76 ☐	91 ☐
2 ☐	17 ☐	32 ☐	47 ☐	62 ☐	77 ☐	92 ☐
3 ☐	18 ☐	33 ☐	48 ☐	63 ☐	78 ☐	93 ☐
4 ☐	19 ☐	34 ☐	49 ☐	64 ☐	79 ☐	94 ☐
5 ☐	20 ☐	35 ☐	50 ☐	65 ☐	80 ☐	95 ☐
6 ☐	21 ☐	36 ☐	51 ☐	66 ☐	81 ☐	96 ☐
7 ☐	22 ☐	37 ☐	52 ☐	67 ☐	82 ☐	97 ☐
8 ☐	23 ☐	38 ☐	53 ☐	68 ☐	83 ☐	98 ☐
9 ☐	24 ☐	39 ☐	54 ☐	69 ☐	84 ☐	☐
10 ☐	25 ☐	40 ☐	55 ☐	70 ☐	85 ☐	☐
11 ☐	26 ☐	41 ☐	56 ☐	71 ☐	86 ☐	☐
12 ☐	27 ☐	42 ☐	57 ☐	72 ☐	87 ☐	☐
13 ☐	28 ☐	43 ☐	58 ☐	73 ☐	88 ☐	☐
14 ☐	29 ☐	44 ☐	59 ☐	74 ☐	89 ☐	☐
15 ☐	30 ☐	45 ☐	60 ☐	75 ☐	90 ☐	☐

CLYDE "BULLDOG" TURNER

OF CARDS I HAVE: ____________

OF CARDS I NEED: ____________

% OF SET FILLED: ____________

KEY CARDS I HAVE: ____________

KEY CARDS I NEED: ____________

COMMENTS: ____________

1948 TOPPS MAGIC (NFL)

1	26	51	76	101	126	151	176	201	226	251
2	27	52	77	102	127	152	177	202	227	252
3	28	53	78	103	128	153	178	203	228	
4	29	54	79	104	129	154	179	204	229	
5	30	55	80	105	130	155	180	205	230	
6	31	56	81	106	131	156	181	206	231	
7	32	57	82	107	132	157	182	207	232	
8	33	58	83	108	133	158	183	208	233	
9	34	59	84	109	134	159	184	209	234	
10	35	60	85	110	135	160	185	210	235	
11	36	61	86	111	136	161	186	211	236	
12	37	62	87	112	137	162	187	212	237	
13	38	63	88	113	138	163	188	213	238	
14	39	64	89	114	139	164	189	214	239	
15	40	65	90	115	140	165	190	215	240	
16	41	66	91	116	141	166	191	216	241	
17	42	67	92	117	142	167	192	217	242	
18	43	68	93	118	143	168	193	218	243	
19	44	69	94	119	144	169	194	219	244	
20	45	70	95	120	145	170	195	220	245	
21	46	71	96	121	146	171	196	221	246	
22	47	72	97	122	147	172	197	222	247	
23	48	73	98	123	148	173	198	223	248	
24	49	74	99	124	149	174	199	224	249	
25	50	75	100	125	150	175	200	225	250	

OF CARDS I HAVE:

OF CARDS I NEED:

% OF SET FILLED:

KEY CARDS I HAVE:

KEY CARDS I NEED:

COMMENTS:

1949 LEAF (NFL)

1 ☐	28 ☐	57 ☐	127 ☐
2 ☐	31 ☐	62 ☐	134 ☐
3 ☐	32 ☐	65 ☐	144 ☐
4 ☐	35 ☐	67 ☐	150 ☐
7 ☐	37 ☐	70 ☐	☐
9 ☐	38 ☐	74 ☐	☐
10 ☐	39 ☐	79 ☐	☐
13 ☐	40 ☐	81 ☐	☐
15 ☐	41 ☐	89 ☐	☐
16 ☐	43 ☐	90 ☐	☐
17 ☐	47 ☐	95 ☐	☐
19 ☐	49 ☐	101 ☐	☐
22 ☐	52 ☐	110 ☐	☐
23 ☐	52 ☐	118 ☐	☐
26 ☐	56 ☐	126 ☐	☐

JOHNNY LUJACK

OF CARDS I HAVE: ____________

OF CARDS I NEED: ____________

% OF SET FILLED: ____________

KEY CARDS I HAVE: ____________

KEY CARDS I NEED: ____________

COMMENTS: ____________

1950 BOWMAN (NFL)

1	26	51	76	101	126
2	27	52	77	102	127
3	28	53	78	103	128
4	29	54	79	104	129
5	30	55	80	105	130
6	31	56	81	106	131
7	32	57	82	107	132
8	33	58	83	108	133
9	34	59	84	109	134
10	35	60	85	110	135
11	36	61	86	111	136
12	37	62	87	112	137
13	38	63	88	113	138
14	39	64	89	114	139
15	40	65	90	115	140
16	41	66	91	116	141
17	42	67	92	117	142
18	43	68	93	118	143
19	44	69	94	119	144
20	45	70	95	120	
21	46	71	96	121	
22	47	72	97	122	
23	48	73	98	123	
24	49	74	99	124	
25	50	75	100	125	

OF CARDS I HAVE: ____________

OF CARDS I NEED: ____________

% OF SET FILLED: ____________

KEY CARDS I HAVE: ____________

KEY CARDS I NEED: ____________

COMMENTS: ____________

1950

1950 BROWNS TEAM ISSUE (NFL)

OF CARDS I HAVE:

OF CARDS I NEED:

% OF SET FILLED:

KEY CARDS I HAVE:

KEY CARDS I NEED:

COMMENTS:

5 Card Set

1950 C.O.P. BETSY ROSS (COLLEGE)

1 ☐ 3 ☐ 5 ☐ ☐
2 ☐ 4 ☐ 6 ☐ ☐

OF CARDS I HAVE:

OF CARDS I NEED:

% OF SET FILLED:

KEY CARDS I HAVE:

KEY CARDS I NEED:

COMMENTS:

6 Card Set

1950 RAMS ADMIRAL (NFL)

1 ☐	9 ☐	17 ☐	25 ☐	33 ☐
2 ☐	10 ☐	18 ☐	26 ☐	34 ☐
3 ☐	11 ☐	19 ☐	27 ☐	35 ☐
4 ☐	12 ☐	20 ☐	28 ☐	☐
5 ☐	13 ☐	21 ☐	29 ☐	☐
6 ☐	14 ☐	22 ☐	30 ☐	☐
7 ☐	15 ☐	23 ☐	31 ☐	☐
8 ☐	16 ☐	24 ☐	32 ☐	☐

OF CARDS I HAVE:

OF CARDS I NEED:

% OF SET FILLED:

KEY CARDS I HAVE:

KEY CARDS I NEED:

COMMENTS:

35 Card Set

1950 TOPPS FELT BACKS (COLLEGE)

1 ☐	16 ☐	31 ☐	46 ☐	61 ☐	76 ☐	91 ☐
2 ☐	17 ☐	32 ☐	47 ☐	62 ☐	77 ☐	92 ☐
3 ☐	18 ☐	33 ☐	48 ☐	63 ☐	78 ☐	93 ☐
4 ☐	19 ☐	34 ☐	49 ☐	64 ☐	79 ☐	94 ☐
5 ☐	20 ☐	35 ☐	50 ☐	65 ☐	80 ☐	95 ☐
6 ☐	21 ☐	36 ☐	51 ☐	66 ☐	81 ☐	96 ☐
7 ☐	22 ☐	37 ☐	52 ☐	67 ☐	82 ☐	97 ☐
8 ☐	23 ☐	38 ☐	53 ☐	68 ☐	83 ☐	98 ☐
9 ☐	24 ☐	39 ☐	54 ☐	69 ☐	84 ☐	99 ☐
10 ☐	25 ☐	40 ☐	55 ☐	70 ☐	85 ☐	100 ☐
11 ☐	26 ☐	41 ☐	56 ☐	71 ☐	86 ☐	☐
12 ☐	27 ☐	42 ☐	57 ☐	72 ☐	87 ☐	☐
13 ☐	28 ☐	43 ☐	58 ☐	73 ☐	88 ☐	☐
14 ☐	29 ☐	44 ☐	59 ☐	74 ☐	89 ☐	☐
15 ☐	30 ☐	45 ☐	60 ☐	75 ☐	90 ☐	☐

FRANK (MOOSE) MILLER
Fleet Halfback
CORNELL

OF CARDS I HAVE: __________

OF CARDS I NEED: __________

% OF SET FILLED: __________

KEY CARDS I HAVE: __________

KEY CARDS I NEED: __________

COMMENTS: __________

1951 BROWNS WHITE BORDER (NFL)

KEY CARDS I HAVE:

OF CARDS I HAVE:

KEY CARDS I NEED:

OF CARDS I NEED:

COMMENTS:

% OF SET FILLED:

25 Card Set

1951 - 52 REDSKINS MATCHBOOKS (NFL)

KEY CARDS I HAVE:

OF CARDS I HAVE:

KEY CARDS I NEED:

OF CARDS I NEED:

COMMENTS:

% OF SET FILLED:

25 Card Set

1951 BOWMAN (NFL)

1 ☐	26 ☐	51 ☐	76 ☐	101 ☐	126 ☐
2 ☐	27 ☐	52 ☐	77 ☐	102 ☐	127 ☐
3 ☐	28 ☐	53 ☐	78 ☐	103 ☐	128 ☐
4 ☐	29 ☐	54 ☐	79 ☐	104 ☐	129 ☐
5 ☐	30 ☐	55 ☐	80 ☐	105 ☐	130 ☐
6 ☐	31 ☐	56 ☐	81 ☐	106 ☐	131 ☐
7 ☐	32 ☐	57 ☐	82 ☐	107 ☐	132 ☐
8 ☐	33 ☐	58 ☐	83 ☐	108 ☐	133 ☐
9 ☐	34 ☐	59 ☐	84 ☐	109 ☐	134 ☐
10 ☐	35 ☐	60 ☐	85 ☐	110 ☐	135 ☐
11 ☐	36 ☐	61 ☐	86 ☐	111 ☐	136 ☐
12 ☐	37 ☐	62 ☐	87 ☐	112 ☐	137 ☐
13 ☐	38 ☐	63 ☐	88 ☐	113 ☐	138 ☐
14 ☐	39 ☐	64 ☐	89 ☐	114 ☐	139 ☐
15 ☐	40 ☐	65 ☐	90 ☐	115 ☐	140 ☐
16 ☐	41 ☐	66 ☐	91 ☐	116 ☐	141 ☐
17 ☐	42 ☐	67 ☐	92 ☐	117 ☐	142 ☐
18 ☐	43 ☐	68 ☐	93 ☐	118 ☐	143 ☐
19 ☐	44 ☐	69 ☐	94 ☐	119 ☐	144 ☐
20 ☐	45 ☐	70 ☐	95 ☐	120 ☐	☐
21 ☐	46 ☐	71 ☐	96 ☐	121 ☐	☐
22 ☐	47 ☐	72 ☐	97 ☐	122 ☐	☐
23 ☐	48 ☐	73 ☐	98 ☐	123 ☐	☐
24 ☐	49 ☐	74 ☐	99 ☐	124 ☐	☐
25 ☐	50 ☐	75 ☐	100 ☐	125 ☐	☐

OF CARDS I HAVE: ____________

OF CARDS I NEED: ____________

% OF SET FILLED: ____________

KEY CARDS I HAVE: ____________

KEY CARDS I NEED: ____________

COMMENTS: ____________

1951 TOPPS MAGIC (COLLEGE)

1 ☐	16 ☐	31 ☐	46 ☐	61 ☐	☐
2 ☐	17 ☐	32 ☐	47 ☐	62 ☐	☐
3 ☐	18 ☐	33 ☐	48 ☐	63 ☐	☐
4 ☐	19 ☐	34 ☐	49 ☐	64 ☐	☐
5 ☐	20 ☐	35 ☐	50 ☐	65 ☐	☐
6 ☐	21 ☐	36 ☐	51 ☐	66 ☐	☐
7 ☐	22 ☐	37 ☐	52 ☐	67 ☐	☐
8 ☐	23 ☐	38 ☐	53 ☐	68 ☐	☐
9 ☐	24 ☐	39 ☐	54 ☐	69 ☐	☐
10 ☐	25 ☐	40 ☐	55 ☐	70 ☐	☐
11 ☐	26 ☐	41 ☐	56 ☐	71 ☐	☐
12 ☐	27 ☐	42 ☐	57 ☐	72 ☐	☐
13 ☐	28 ☐	43 ☐	58 ☐	73 ☐	☐
14 ☐	29 ☐	44 ☐	59 ☐	74 ☐	☐
15 ☐	30 ☐	45 ☐	60 ☐	75 ☐	☐

DICK HIGHTOWER
CENTER (MUSTANGS)

OF CARDS I HAVE: ______

OF CARDS I NEED: ______

% OF SET FILLED: ______

KEY CARDS I HAVE: ______

KEY CARDS I NEED: ______

COMMENTS: ______

1952

1952 Bread For Health (NFL)

Key cards I have:

Key cards I need:

Comments:

# of cards I have:

# of cards I need:

% of set filled:

32 Card Set

1952 Crown Brand (CFL)

1	11	21	31	41
2	12	22	32	42
3	13	23	33	43
4	14	24	34	44
5	15	25	35	45
6	16	26	36	46
7	17	27	37	47
8	18	28	38	48
9	19	29	39	
10	20	30	40	

Key cards I have:

Key cards I need:

Comments:

# of cards I have:

# of cards I need:

% of set filled:

48 Card Set

1952 BOWMAN LARGE (NFL)

1 ☐	26 ☐	51 ☐	76 ☐	101 ☐	126 ☐
2 ☐	27 ☐	52 ☐	77 ☐	102 ☐	127 ☐
3 ☐	28 ☐	53 ☐	78 ☐	103 ☐	128 ☐
4 ☐	29 ☐	54 ☐	79 ☐	104 ☐	129 ☐
5 ☐	30 ☐	55 ☐	80 ☐	105 ☐	130 ☐
6 ☐	31 ☐	56 ☐	81 ☐	106 ☐	131 ☐
7 ☐	32 ☐	57 ☐	82 ☐	107 ☐	132 ☐
8 ☐	33 ☐	58 ☐	83 ☐	108 ☐	133 ☐
9 ☐	34 ☐	59 ☐	84 ☐	109 ☐	134 ☐
10 ☐	35 ☐	60 ☐	85 ☐	110 ☐	135 ☐
11 ☐	36 ☐	61 ☐	86 ☐	111 ☐	136 ☐
12 ☐	37 ☐	62 ☐	87 ☐	112 ☐	137 ☐
13 ☐	38 ☐	63 ☐	88 ☐	113 ☐	138 ☐
14 ☐	39 ☐	64 ☐	89 ☐	114 ☐	139 ☐
15 ☐	40 ☐	65 ☐	90 ☐	115 ☐	140 ☐
16 ☐	41 ☐	66 ☐	91 ☐	116 ☐	141 ☐
17 ☐	42 ☐	67 ☐	92 ☐	117 ☐	142 ☐
18 ☐	43 ☐	68 ☐	93 ☐	118 ☐	143 ☐
19 ☐	44 ☐	69 ☐	94 ☐	119 ☐	144 ☐
20 ☐	45 ☐	70 ☐	95 ☐	120 ☐	☐
21 ☐	46 ☐	71 ☐	96 ☐	121 ☐	☐
22 ☐	47 ☐	72 ☐	97 ☐	122 ☐	☐
23 ☐	48 ☐	73 ☐	98 ☐	123 ☐	☐
24 ☐	49 ☐	74 ☐	99 ☐	124 ☐	☐
25 ☐	50 ☐	75 ☐	100 ☐	125 ☐	☐

GEORGE S. HALAS

OF CARDS I HAVE: ____________

OF CARDS I NEED: ____________

% OF SET FILLED: ____________

KEY CARDS I HAVE: ____________

KEY CARDS I NEED: ____________

COMMENTS: ____________

1952 BOWMAN SMALL (NFL)

1	26	51	76	101	126
2	27	52	77	102	127
3	28	53	78	103	128
4	29	54	79	104	129
5	30	55	80	105	130
6	31	56	81	106	131
7	32	57	82	107	132
8	33	58	83	108	133
9	34	59	84	109	134
10	35	60	85	110	135
11	36	61	86	111	136
12	37	62	87	112	137
13	38	63	88	113	138
14	39	64	89	114	139
15	40	65	90	115	140
16	41	66	91	116	141
17	42	67	92	117	142
18	43	68	93	118	143
19	44	69	94	119	144
20	45	70	95	120	
21	46	71	96	121	
22	47	72	97	122	
23	48	73	98	123	
24	49	74	99	124	
25	50	75	100	125	

NORMAN VAN BROCKLIN

OF CARDS I HAVE: ____________

OF CARDS I NEED: ____________

% OF SET FILLED: ____________

KEY CARDS I HAVE: ____________

KEY CARDS I NEED: ____________

COMMENTS: ____________

1952 PARKHURST (CFL)

1 ☐	26 ☐	51 ☐	76 ☐	
2 ☐	27 ☐	52 ☐	77 ☐	
3 ☐	28 ☐	53 ☐	78 ☐	
4 ☐	29 ☐	54 ☐	79 ☐	
5 ☐	30 ☐	55 ☐	80 ☐	
6 ☐	31 ☐	56 ☐	81 ☐	
7 ☐	32 ☐	57 ☐	82 ☐	
8 ☐	33 ☐	58 ☐	83 ☐	
9 ☐	34 ☐	59 ☐	84 ☐	
10 ☐	35 ☐	60 ☐	85 ☐	
11 ☐	36 ☐	61 ☐	86 ☐	
12 ☐	37 ☐	62 ☐	87 ☐	
13 ☐	38 ☐	63 ☐	88 ☐	
14 ☐	39 ☐	64 ☐	89 ☐	
15 ☐	40 ☐	65 ☐	90 ☐	☐
16 ☐	41 ☐	66 ☐	91 ☐	☐
17 ☐	42 ☐	67 ☐	92 ☐	☐
18 ☐	43 ☐	68 ☐	93 ☐	☐
19 ☐	44 ☐	69 ☐	94 ☐	☐
20 ☐	45 ☐	70 ☐	95 ☐	☐
21 ☐	46 ☐	71 ☐	96 ☐	☐
22 ☐	47 ☐	72 ☐	97 ☐	☐
23 ☐	48 ☐	73 ☐	98 ☐	☐
24 ☐	49 ☐	74 ☐	99 ☐	☐
25 ☐	50 ☐	75 ☐	100 ☐	☐

OF CARDS I HAVE: ______________

OF CARDS I NEED: ______________

% OF SET FILLED: ______________

KEY CARDS I HAVE: ______________

KEY CARDS I NEED: ______________

COMMENTS: ______________

1953

1953 Oregon (College)

1 2 3 4 5 6 7 8 9 10 11 12 13 14 15 16 17 18 19 20

Key cards I have:

Key cards I need:

Comments:

# of cards I have:

# of cards I need:

% of set filled:

20 Card Set

1953 Rams Black Border (NFL)

Key cards I have:

Key cards I need:

Comments:

# of cards I have:

# of cards I need:

% of set filled:

36 Card Set

1953 BOWMAN (NFL)

1 ☐	16 ☐	31 ☐	46 ☐	61 ☐	76 ☐	91 ☐
2 ☐	17 ☐	32 ☐	47 ☐	62 ☐	77 ☐	92 ☐
3 ☐	18 ☐	33 ☐	48 ☐	63 ☐	78 ☐	93 ☐
4 ☐	19 ☐	34 ☐	49 ☐	64 ☐	79 ☐	94 ☐
5 ☐	20 ☐	35 ☐	50 ☐	65 ☐	80 ☐	95 ☐
6 ☐	21 ☐	36 ☐	51 ☐	66 ☐	81 ☐	96 ☐
7 ☐	22 ☐	37 ☐	52 ☐	67 ☐	82 ☐	☐
8 ☐	23 ☐	38 ☐	53 ☐	68 ☐	83 ☐	☐
9 ☐	24 ☐	39 ☐	54 ☐	69 ☐	84 ☐	☐
10 ☐	25 ☐	40 ☐	55 ☐	70 ☐	85 ☐	☐
11 ☐	26 ☐	41 ☐	56 ☐	71 ☐	86 ☐	☐
12 ☐	27 ☐	42 ☐	57 ☐	72 ☐	87 ☐	☐
13 ☐	28 ☐	43 ☐	58 ☐	73 ☐	88 ☐	☐
14 ☐	29 ☐	44 ☐	59 ☐	74 ☐	89 ☐	☐
15 ☐	30 ☐	45 ☐	60 ☐	75 ☐	90 ☐	☐

OTTO GRAHAM
BROWNS

OF CARDS I HAVE: ______________

OF CARDS I NEED: ______________

% OF SET FILLED: ______________

KEY CARDS I HAVE: ____________________

____

____

____

____

____

____

KEY CARDS I NEED: ____________________

____

____

____

____

COMMENTS: ____________________

____

____

____

____

1954 AND 55

1954 RAMS BLACK BORDER (NFL)

KEY CARDS I HAVE:

KEY CARDS I NEED:

COMMENTS:

OF CARDS I HAVE:

OF CARDS I NEED:

% OF SET FILLED:

36 Card Set

1954-55 BROWNS WHITE BORDER (NFL)

KEY CARDS I HAVE:

KEY CARDS I NEED:

COMMENTS:

OF CARDS I HAVE:

OF CARDS I NEED:

% OF SET FILLED:

20 Card Set

1954 BLUE RIBBON TEA (CFL)

1 ☐	16 ☐	31 ☐	46 ☐	61 ☐	76 ☐
2 ☐	17 ☐	32 ☐	47 ☐	62 ☐	77 ☐
3 ☐	18 ☐	33 ☐	48 ☐	63 ☐	78 ☐
4 ☐	19 ☐	34 ☐	49 ☐	64 ☐	79 ☐
5 ☐	20 ☐	35 ☐	50 ☐	65 ☐	80 ☐
6 ☐	21 ☐	36 ☐	51 ☐	66 ☐	☐
7 ☐	22 ☐	37 ☐	52 ☐	67 ☐	☐
8 ☐	23 ☐	38 ☐	53 ☐	68 ☐	☐
9 ☐	24 ☐	39 ☐	54 ☐	69 ☐	☐
10 ☐	25 ☐	40 ☐	55 ☐	70 ☐	☐
11 ☐	26 ☐	41 ☐	56 ☐	71 ☐	☐
12 ☐	27 ☐	42 ☐	57 ☐	72 ☐	☐
13 ☐	28 ☐	43 ☐	58 ☐	73 ☐	☐
14 ☐	29 ☐	44 ☐	59 ☐	74 ☐	☐
15 ☐	30 ☐	45 ☐	60 ☐	75 ☐	☐

OF CARDS I HAVE: __________

OF CARDS I NEED: __________

% OF SET FILLED: __________

KEY CARDS I HAVE:

KEY CARDS I NEED:

COMMENTS:

1954 BOWMAN (NFL)

1 ☐	26 ☐	51 ☐	76 ☐	101 ☐	126 ☐
2 ☐	27 ☐	52 ☐	77 ☐	102 ☐	127 ☐
3 ☐	28 ☐	53 ☐	78 ☐	103 ☐	128 ☐
4 ☐	29 ☐	54 ☐	79 ☐	104 ☐	
5 ☐	30 ☐	55 ☐	80 ☐	105 ☐	
6 ☐	31 ☐	56 ☐	81 ☐	106 ☐	
7 ☐	32 ☐	57 ☐	82 ☐	107 ☐	
8 ☐	33 ☐	58 ☐	83 ☐	108 ☐	
9 ☐	34 ☐	59 ☐	84 ☐	109 ☐	
10 ☐	35 ☐	60 ☐	85 ☐	110 ☐	
11 ☐	36 ☐	61 ☐	86 ☐	111 ☐	
12 ☐	37 ☐	62 ☐	87 ☐	112 ☐	
13 ☐	38 ☐	63 ☐	88 ☐	113 ☐	
14 ☐	39 ☐	64 ☐	89 ☐	114 ☐	
15 ☐	40 ☐	65 ☐	90 ☐	115 ☐	
16 ☐	41 ☐	66 ☐	91 ☐	116 ☐	
17 ☐	42 ☐	67 ☐	92 ☐	117 ☐	
18 ☐	43 ☐	68 ☐	93 ☐	118 ☐	
19 ☐	44 ☐	69 ☐	94 ☐	119 ☐	
20 ☐	45 ☐	70 ☐	95 ☐	120 ☐	
21 ☐	46 ☐	71 ☐	96 ☐	121 ☐	
22 ☐	47 ☐	72 ☐	97 ☐	122 ☐	
23 ☐	48 ☐	73 ☐	98 ☐	123 ☐	
24 ☐	49 ☐	74 ☐	99 ☐	124 ☐	
25 ☐	50 ☐	75 ☐	100 ☐	125 ☐	

CHUCK BEDNARIK
PHILADELPHIA EAGLES

OF CARDS I HAVE: ____________

OF CARDS I NEED: ____________

% OF SET FILLED: ____________

KEY CARDS I HAVE: ____________________

KEY CARDS I NEED: ____________________

COMMENTS: ____________________

1955 BROWNS CARLING BEER (NFL)

1 2 3 4 5 6 7 8 9 10

KEY CARDS I HAVE:

KEY CARDS I NEED:

COMMENTS:

\# OF CARDS I HAVE:

\# OF CARDS I NEED:

% OF SET FILLED:

10 Card Set

1955 49ERS WHITE BORDER (NFL)

KEY CARDS I HAVE:

KEY CARDS I NEED:

COMMENTS:

\# OF CARDS I HAVE:

\# OF CARDS I NEED:

% OF SET FILLED:

38 Card Set

1955 BROWNS COLOR POSTCARDS (NFL)

KEY CARDS I HAVE:

KEY CARDS I NEED:

COMMENTS:

OF CARDS I HAVE:

OF CARDS I NEED:

% OF SET FILLED:

6 Card Set

1955 RAMS BLACK BORDER (NFL)

KEY CARDS I HAVE:

KEY CARDS I NEED:

COMMENTS:

OF CARDS I HAVE:

OF CARDS I NEED:

% OF SET FILLED:

37 Card Set

1955 BOWMAN (NFL)

1 ☐	26 ☐	51 ☐	76 ☐	101 ☐	126 ☐	151 ☐
2 ☐	27 ☐	52 ☐	77 ☐	102 ☐	127 ☐	152 ☐
3 ☐	28 ☐	53 ☐	78 ☐	103 ☐	128 ☐	153 ☐
4 ☐	29 ☐	54 ☐	79 ☐	104 ☐	129 ☐	154 ☐
5 ☐	30 ☐	55 ☐	80 ☐	105 ☐	130 ☐	155 ☐
6 ☐	31 ☐	56 ☐	81 ☐	106 ☐	131 ☐	156 ☐
7 ☐	32 ☐	57 ☐	82 ☐	107 ☐	132 ☐	157 ☐
8 ☐	33 ☐	58 ☐	83 ☐	108 ☐	133 ☐	158 ☐
9 ☐	34 ☐	59 ☐	84 ☐	109 ☐	134 ☐	159 ☐
10 ☐	35 ☐	60 ☐	85 ☐	110 ☐	135 ☐	160 ☐
11 ☐	36 ☐	61 ☐	86 ☐	111 ☐	136 ☐	☐
12 ☐	37 ☐	62 ☐	87 ☐	112 ☐	137 ☐	☐
13 ☐	38 ☐	63 ☐	88 ☐	113 ☐	138 ☐	☐
14 ☐	39 ☐	64 ☐	89 ☐	114 ☐	139 ☐	☐
15 ☐	40 ☐	65 ☐	90 ☐	115 ☐	140 ☐	☐
16 ☐	41 ☐	66 ☐	91 ☐	116 ☐	141 ☐	☐
17 ☐	42 ☐	67 ☐	92 ☐	117 ☐	142 ☐	☐
18 ☐	43 ☐	68 ☐	93 ☐	118 ☐	143 ☐	☐
19 ☐	44 ☐	69 ☐	94 ☐	119 ☐	144 ☐	☐
20 ☐	45 ☐	70 ☐	95 ☐	120 ☐	145 ☐	☐
21 ☐	46 ☐	71 ☐	96 ☐	121 ☐	146 ☐	☐
22 ☐	47 ☐	72 ☐	97 ☐	122 ☐	147 ☐	☐
23 ☐	48 ☐	73 ☐	98 ☐	123 ☐	148 ☐	☐
24 ☐	49 ☐	74 ☐	99 ☐	124 ☐	149 ☐	☐
25 ☐	50 ☐	75 ☐	100 ☐	125 ☐	150 ☐	☐

OF CARDS I HAVE: ____________

OF CARDS I NEED: ____________

% OF SET FILLED: ____________

KEY CARDS I HAVE: ____________

KEY CARDS I NEED: ____________

COMMENTS: ____________

1955 TOPPS ALL-AMERICAN (COLLEGE)

1 ☐	16 ☐	31 ☐	46 ☐	61 ☐	76 ☐	91 ☐
2 ☐	17 ☐	32 ☐	47 ☐	62 ☐	77 ☐	92 ☐
3 ☐	18 ☐	33 ☐	48 ☐	63 ☐	78 ☐	93 ☐
4 ☐	19 ☐	34 ☐	49 ☐	64 ☐	79 ☐	94 ☐
5 ☐	20 ☐	35 ☐	50 ☐	65 ☐	80 ☐	95 ☐
6 ☐	21 ☐	36 ☐	51 ☐	66 ☐	81 ☐	96 ☐
7 ☐	22 ☐	37 ☐	52 ☐	67 ☐	82 ☐	97 ☐
8 ☐	23 ☐	38 ☐	53 ☐	68 ☐	83 ☐	98 ☐
9 ☐	24 ☐	39 ☐	54 ☐	69 ☐	84 ☐	99 ☐
10 ☐	25 ☐	40 ☐	55 ☐	70 ☐	85 ☐	100 ☐
11 ☐	26 ☐	41 ☐	56 ☐	71 ☐	86 ☐	
12 ☐	27 ☐	42 ☐	57 ☐	72 ☐	87 ☐	
13 ☐	28 ☐	43 ☐	58 ☐	73 ☐	88 ☐	
14 ☐	29 ☐	44 ☐	59 ☐	74 ☐	89 ☐	
15 ☐	30 ☐	45 ☐	60 ☐	75 ☐	90 ☐	

"RED" GRANGE Quarterback

OF CARDS I HAVE: ____________

OF CARDS I NEED: ____________

% OF SET FILLED: ____________

KEY CARDS I HAVE: ____________

KEY CARDS I NEED: ____________

COMMENTS: ____________

1956

1956 49ERS WHITE BORDER (NFL)

1 ☐	8 ☐	15 ☐	22 ☐	29 ☐
2 ☐	9 ☐	16 ☐	23 ☐	☐
3 ☐	10 ☐	17 ☐	24 ☐	☐
4 ☐	11 ☐	18 ☐	25 ☐	☐
5 ☐	12 ☐	19 ☐	26 ☐	☐
6 ☐	13 ☐	20 ☐	27 ☐	☐
7 ☐	14 ☐	21 ☐	28 ☐	☐

KEY CARDS I HAVE:

OF CARDS I HAVE:

KEY CARDS I NEED:

OF CARDS I NEED:

COMMENTS:

% OF SET FILLED:

29 Card Set

1956 GIANTS TEAM ISSUE (NFL)

KEY CARDS I HAVE:

OF CARDS I HAVE:

KEY CARDS I NEED:

OF CARDS I NEED:

COMMENTS:

% OF SET FILLED:

36 Card Set

1956 RAMS WHITE BORDER (NFL)

KEY CARDS I HAVE: # OF CARDS I HAVE:

KEY CARDS I NEED: # OF CARDS I NEED:

COMMENTS: % OF SET FILLED:

37 Card Set

1956 OREGON (COLLEGE)

1 6 11 16
2 7 12 17
3 8 13 18
4 9 14 19
5 10 15

KEY CARDS I HAVE: # OF CARDS I HAVE:

KEY CARDS I NEED: # OF CARDS I NEED:

COMMENTS: % OF SET FILLED:

19 Card Set

1956 PARKHURST (CFL)

1 ☐	16 ☐	31 ☐	46 ☐
2 ☐	17 ☐	32 ☐	47 ☐
3 ☐	18 ☐	33 ☐	48 ☐
4 ☐	19 ☐	34 ☐	49 ☐
5 ☐	20 ☐	35 ☐	50 ☐
6 ☐	21 ☐	36 ☐	☐
7 ☐	22 ☐	37 ☐	☐
8 ☐	23 ☐	38 ☐	☐
9 ☐	24 ☐	39 ☐	☐
10 ☐	25 ☐	40 ☐	☐
11 ☐	26 ☐	41 ☐	☐
12 ☐	27 ☐	42 ☐	☐
13 ☐	28 ☐	43 ☐	☐
14 ☐	29 ☐	44 ☐	☐
15 ☐	30 ☐	45 ☐	☐

OF CARDS I HAVE: ____________

OF CARDS I NEED: ____________

% OF SET FILLED: ____________

KEY CARDS I HAVE: ____________

KEY CARDS I NEED: ____________

COMMENTS: ____________

1956 SHREDDED WHEAT (CFL)

A1 ☐	B1 ☐	C1 ☐	D1 ☐	E1 ☐	F1 ☐	G1 ☐	☐
A2 ☐	B2 ☐	C2 ☐	D2 ☐	E2 ☐	F2 ☐	G2 ☐	☐
A3 ☐	B3 ☐	C3 ☐	D3 ☐	E3 ☐	F3 ☐	G3 ☐	☐
A4 ☐	B4 ☐	C4 ☐	D4 ☐	E4 ☐	F4 ☐	G4 ☐	☐
A5 ☐	B5 ☐	C5 ☐	D5 ☐	E5 ☐	F5 ☐	G5 ☐	☐
A6 ☐	B6 ☐	C6 ☐	D6 ☐	E6 ☐	F6 ☐	G6 ☐	☐
A7 ☐	B7 ☐	C7 ☐	D7 ☐	E7 ☐	F7 ☐	G7 ☐	☐
A8 ☐	B8 ☐	C8 ☐	D8 ☐	E8 ☐	F8 ☐	G8 ☐	☐
A9 ☐	B9 ☐	C9 ☐	D9 ☐	E9 ☐	F9 ☐	G9 ☐	☐
A10 ☐	B10 ☐	C10 ☐	D10 ☐	E10 ☐	F10 ☐	G10 ☐	☐
A11 ☐	B11 ☐	C11 ☐	D11 ☐	E11 ☐	F11 ☐	G11 ☐	☐
A12 ☐	B12 ☐	C12 ☐	D12 ☐	E12 ☐	F12 ☐	G12 ☐	☐
A13 ☐	B13 ☐	C13 ☐	D13 ☐	E13 ☐	F13 ☐	G13 ☐	☐
A14 ☐	B14 ☐	C14 ☐	D14 ☐	E14 ☐	F14 ☐	G14 ☐	☐
A15 ☐	B15 ☐	C15 ☐	D15 ☐	E15 ☐	F15 ☐	G15 ☐	☐

12 B JACK PARKER

OF CARDS I HAVE: ____________

OF CARDS I NEED: ____________

% OF SET FILLED: ____________

KEY CARDS I HAVE: ____________

KEY CARDS I NEED: ____________

COMMENTS: ____________

1956 Topps (NFL)

1	26	51	76	101
2	27	52	77	102
3	28	53	78	103
4	29	54	79	104
5	30	55	80	105
6	31	56	81	106
7	32	57	82	107
8	33	58	83	108
9	34	59	84	109
10	35	60	85	110
11	36	61	86	111
12	37	62	87	112
13	38	63	88	113
14	39	64	89	114
15	40	65	90	115
16	41	66	91	116
17	42	67	92	117
18	43	68	93	118
19	44	69	94	119
20	45	70	95	120
21	46	71	96	
22	47	72	97	
23	48	73	98	
24	49	74	99	
25	50	75	100	

GIANTS

Frank Gifford

HALFBACK NEW YORK GIANTS

OF CARDS I HAVE:

OF CARDS I NEED:

% OF SET FILLED:

KEY CARDS I HAVE:

KEY CARDS I NEED:

COMMENTS:

1957 49ERS WHITE BORDER (NFL)

1 ☐	8 ☐	17 ☐	25 ☐	33 ☐	41 ☐
2 ☐	10 ☐	18 ☐	26 ☐	34 ☐	42 ☐
3 ☐	11 ☐	19 ☐	27 ☐	35 ☐	43 ☐
4 ☐	12 ☐	20 ☐	28 ☐	36 ☐	☐
5 ☐	13 ☐	21 ☐	29 ☐	37 ☐	☐
6 ☐	14 ☐	22 ☐	30 ☐	38 ☐	☐
7 ☐	15 ☐	23 ☐	31 ☐	39 ☐	☐
8 ☐	16 ☐	24 ☐	32 ☐	40 ☐	☐

KEY CARDS I HAVE: ____________________

KEY CARDS I NEED: ____________________

COMMENTS: ____________________

OF CARDS I HAVE: ____________

OF CARDS I NEED: ____________

% OF SET FILLED: ____________

43 Card Set

1957 GIANT'S TEAM ISSUE (NFL)

KEY CARDS I HAVE: ____________________

KEY CARDS I NEED: ____________________

COMMENTS: ____________________

OF CARDS I HAVE: ____________

OF CARDS I NEED: ____________

% OF SET FILLED: ____________

40 Card Set

1957 RAMS BLACK BORDER (NFL)

OF CARDS I HAVE:

KEY CARDS I HAVE:

OF CARDS I NEED:

% OF SET FILLED:

KEY CARDS I NEED:

COMMENTS:

NOTES

NOTES

1957 Topps (NFL)

1 ☐	26 ☐	51 ☐	76 ☐	101 ☐	126 ☐	
2 ☐	27 ☐	52 ☐	77 ☐	102 ☐	127 ☐	
3 ☐	28 ☐	53 ☐	78 ☐	103 ☐	128 ☐	
4 ☐	29 ☐	54 ☐	79 ☐	104 ☐	129 ☐	
5 ☐	30 ☐	55 ☐	80 ☐	105 ☐	130 ☐	
6 ☐	31 ☐	56 ☐	81 ☐	106 ☐	131 ☐	
7 ☐	32 ☐	57 ☐	82 ☐	107 ☐	132 ☐	
8 ☐	33 ☐	58 ☐	83 ☐	108 ☐	133 ☐	
9 ☐	34 ☐	59 ☐	84 ☐	109 ☐	134 ☐	
10 ☐	35 ☐	60 ☐	85 ☐	110 ☐	135 ☐	
11 ☐	36 ☐	61 ☐	86 ☐	111 ☐	136 ☐	151 ☐
12 ☐	37 ☐	62 ☐	87 ☐	112 ☐	137 ☐	152 ☐
13 ☐	38 ☐	63 ☐	88 ☐	113 ☐	138 ☐	153 ☐
14 ☐	39 ☐	64 ☐	89 ☐	114 ☐	139 ☐	154 ☐
15 ☐	40 ☐	65 ☐	90 ☐	115 ☐	140 ☐	☐
16 ☐	41 ☐	66 ☐	91 ☐	116 ☐	141 ☐	☐
17 ☐	42 ☐	67 ☐	92 ☐	117 ☐	142 ☐	☐
18 ☐	43 ☐	68 ☐	93 ☐	118 ☐	143 ☐	☐
19 ☐	44 ☐	69 ☐	94 ☐	119 ☐	144 ☐	☐
20 ☐	45 ☐	70 ☐	95 ☐	120 ☐	145 ☐	☐
21 ☐	46 ☐	71 ☐	96 ☐	121 ☐	146 ☐	☐
22 ☐	47 ☐	72 ☐	97 ☐	122 ☐	147 ☐	☐
23 ☐	48 ☐	73 ☐	98 ☐	123 ☐	148 ☐	☐
24 ☐	49 ☐	74 ☐	99 ☐	124 ☐	149 ☐	☐
25 ☐	50 ☐	75 ☐	100 ☐	125 ☐	150 ☐	☐

OF CARDS I HAVE: ______________

OF CARDS I NEED: ______________

% OF SET FILLED: ______________

KEY CARDS I HAVE: ______________________________

KEY CARDS I NEED: ______________________________

COMMENTS: ______________________________

1958

1958 49ERS WHITE BORDER (NFL)

1	11	21	31	41
2	12	22	32	42
3	13	23	33	43
4	14	24	34	44
5	15	25	35	
6	16	26	36	
7	17	27	37	
8	18	28	38	
9	19	29	39	
10	20	30	40	

KEY CARDS I HAVE: # OF CARDS I HAVE:

KEY CARDS I NEED: # OF CARDS I NEED:

COMMENTS: % OF SET FILLED:

44 Card Set

1958 OREGON (COLLEGE)

1	6	11	16	
2	7	12	17	
3	8	13	18	
4	9	14	19	
5	10	15	20	

KEY CARDS I HAVE: # OF CARDS I HAVE:

KEY CARDS I NEED: # OF CARDS I NEED:

COMMENTS: % OF SET FILLED:

20 Card Set

1958 TOPPS (CFL)

1	16	31	46	61	76
2	17	32	47	62	77
3	18	33	48	63	78
4	19	34	49	64	79
5	20	35	50	65	80
6	21	36	51	66	81
7	22	37	52	67	82
8	23	38	53	68	83
9	24	39	54	69	84
10	25	40	55	70	85
11	26	41	56	71	86
12	27	42	57	72	87
13	28	43	58	73	88
14	29	44	59	74	
15	30	45	60	75	

JOHN BARROW
TACKLE HAMILTON TIGER CATS

OF CARDS I HAVE:

OF CARDS I NEED:

% OF SET FILLED:

KEY CARDS I HAVE:

KEY CARDS I NEED:

COMMENTS:

1958 Topps (NFL)

1	26	51	76	101	126
2	27	52	77	102	127
3	28	53	78	103	128
4	29	54	79	104	129
5	30	55	80	105	130
6	31	56	81	106	131
7	32	57	82	107	132
8	33	58	83	108	
9	34	59	84	109	
10	35	60	85	110	
11	36	61	86	111	
12	37	62	87	112	
13	38	63	88	113	
14	39	64	89	114	
15	40	65	90	115	
16	41	66	91	116	
17	42	67	92	117	
18	43	68	93	118	
19	44	69	94	119	
20	45	70	95	120	
21	46	71	96	121	
22	47	72	97	122	
23	48	73	98	123	
24	49	74	99	124	
25	50	75	100	125	

JIMMY BROWN
FULLBACK CLEVELAND BROWNS

\# OF CARDS I HAVE:

\# OF CARDS I NEED:

% OF SET FILLED:

KEY CARDS I HAVE:

KEY CARDS I NEED:

COMMENTS:

1958 - 59 REDSKINS MATCHBOOKS (NFL)

KEY CARDS I HAVE:

KEY CARDS I NEED:

COMMENTS:

OF CARDS I HAVE:

OF CARDS I NEED:

% OF SET FILLED:

20 Card Set

1959 BROWN'S CARLING BEER (NFL)

A
B
C
E
F
G
J
K

KEY CARDS I HAVE:

KEY CARDS I NEED:

COMMENTS:

OF CARDS I HAVE:

OF CARDS I NEED:

% OF SET FILLED:

9 Card Set

1959

1959 BAZOOKA (NFL)

KEY CARDS I HAVE:

KEY CARDS I NEED:

COMMENTS:

OF CARDS I HAVE:

OF CARDS I NEED:

% OF SET FILLED:

18 Card Set

1959 EAGLE'S JAY PUBLISHING (NFL)

KEY CARDS I HAVE:

KEY CARDS I NEED:

COMMENTS:

OF CARDS I HAVE:

OF CARDS I NEED:

% OF SET FILLED:

12 Card Set

1959 49ER'S WHITE BORDER (NFL)

1 2 3 4 5 6 7 8 9 10
11 12 13 14 15 16 17 18 19 20
21 22 23 24 25 26 27 28 29 30
31 32 33 34 35 36 37 38 39 40
41 42 43 44 45

KEY CARDS I HAVE:

OF CARDS I HAVE:

KEY CARDS I NEED:

OF CARDS I NEED:

COMMENTS:

% OF SET FILLED:

45 Card Set

1959 KAHN'S (NFL)

KEY CARDS I HAVE:

OF CARDS I HAVE:

KEY CARDS I NEED:

OF CARDS I NEED:

COMMENTS:

% OF SET FILLED:

31 Card Set

1959 SAN GIORGIO FLIPBOOKS (NFL)

1 ☐	5 ☐	9 ☐	13 ☐	17 ☐
2 ☐	6 ☐	10 ☐	14 ☐	☐
3 ☐	7 ☐	11 ☐	15 ☐	☐
4 ☐	8 ☐	12 ☐	16 ☐	☐

KEY CARDS I HAVE: ______

\# OF CARDS I HAVE: ______

KEY CARDS I NEED: ______

\# OF CARDS I NEED: ______

COMMENTS: ______

% OF SET FILLED: ______

17 Card Set

1959 RAMS BELL BRAND (NFL)

1 ☐	11 ☐	21 ☐	31 ☐	☐
2 ☐	12 ☐	22 ☐	32 ☐	☐
3 ☐	13 ☐	23 ☐	33 ☐	☐
4 ☐	14 ☐	24 ☐	34 ☐	☐
5 ☐	15 ☐	25 ☐	35 ☐	☐
6 ☐	16 ☐	26 ☐	36 ☐	☐
7 ☐	17 ☐	27 ☐	37 ☐	☐
8 ☐	18 ☐	28 ☐	38 ☐	☐
9 ☐	19 ☐	29 ☐	39 ☐	☐
10 ☐	20 ☐	30 ☐	40 ☐	☐

JACK PARDEE
Linebacker L.A. Rams

KEY CARDS I HAVE: ______

\# OF CARDS I HAVE: ______

KEY CARDS I NEED: ______

\# OF CARDS I NEED: ______

COMMENTS: ______

% OF SET FILLED: ______

40 Card Set

1959 TOPPS (CFL)

1	16	31	46	61	76
2	17	32	47	62	77
3	18	33	48	63	78
4	19	34	49	64	79
5	20	35	50	65	80
6	21	36	51	66	81
7	22	37	52	67	82
8	23	38	53	68	83
9	24	39	54	69	84
10	25	40	55	70	85
11	26	41	56	71	86
12	27	42	57	72	87
13	28	43	58	73	88
14	29	44	59	74	
15	30	45	60	75	

ESKIMO

DON BARRY

CENTER EDMONTON ESKIMOS

OF CARDS I HAVE:

OF CARDS I NEED:

% OF SET FILLED:

KEY CARDS I HAVE:

KEY CARDS I NEED:

COMMENTS:

1959 Topps (NFL)

1	26	51	76	101	126	151	
2	27	52	77	102	127	152	
3	28	53	78	103	128	153	
4	29	54	79	104	129	154	
5	30	55	80	105	130	155	
6	31	56	81	106	131	156	
7	32	57	82	107	132	157	
8	33	58	83	108	133	158	
9	34	59	84	109	134	159	
10	35	60	85	110	135	160	
11	36	61	86	111	136	161	
12	37	62	87	112	137	162	
13	38	63	88	113	138	163	
14	39	64	89	114	139	164	
15	40	65	90	115	140	165	176
16	41	66	91	116	141	166	
17	42	67	92	117	142	167	
18	43	68	93	118	143	168	
19	44	69	94	119	144	169	
20	45	70	95	120	145	170	
21	46	71	96	121	146	171	
22	47	72	97	122	147	172	
23	48	73	98	123	148	173	
24	49	74	99	124	149	174	
25	50	75	100	125	150	175	

Y. A. TITTLE
QUARTERBACK SAN FRANCISCO 49'ERS

OF CARDS I HAVE: ______________

OF CARDS I NEED: ______________

% OF SET FILLED: ______________

KEY CARDS I HAVE: ______________

KEY CARDS I NEED: ______________

COMMENTS: ______________

1959 WHEATIE'S (CFL)

1 ☐	16 ☐	31 ☐	46 ☐
2 ☐	17 ☐	32 ☐	47 ☐
3 ☐	18 ☐	33 ☐	48 ☐
4 ☐	19 ☐	34 ☐	
5 ☐	20 ☐	35 ☐	
6 ☐	21 ☐	36 ☐	
7 ☐	22 ☐	37 ☐	
8 ☐	23 ☐	38 ☐	
9 ☐	24 ☐	39 ☐	
10 ☐	25 ☐	40 ☐	
11 ☐	26 ☐	41 ☐	
12 ☐	27 ☐	42 ☐	
13 ☐	28 ☐	43 ☐	
14 ☐	29 ☐	44 ☐	
15 ☐	30 ☐	45 ☐	

OF CARDS I HAVE: ________

OF CARDS I NEED: ________

% OF SET FILLED: ________

KEY CARDS I HAVE: ________

KEY CARDS I NEED: ________

COMMENTS: ________

1960

1960 BILLS TEAM ISSUE (AFL)

KEY CARDS I HAVE:

OF CARDS I HAVE:

KEY CARDS I NEED:

OF CARDS I NEED:

COMMENTS:

% OF SET FILLED:

40 Card Set

1960 CARDINALS MAYROSE FRANKS (NFL)

1
2
3
4
5
6
7
8
9
10
11

KEY CARDS I HAVE:

OF CARDS I HAVE:

KEY CARDS I NEED:

OF CARDS I NEED:

COMMENTS:

% OF SET FILLED:

11 Card Set

1960 FLEER (AFL)

1 ☐	26 ☐	51 ☐	76 ☐	101 ☐	126 ☐
2 ☐	27 ☐	52 ☐	77 ☐	102 ☐	127 ☐
3 ☐	28 ☐	53 ☐	78 ☐	103 ☐	128 ☐
4 ☐	29 ☐	54 ☐	79 ☐	104 ☐	129 ☐
5 ☐	30 ☐	55 ☐	80 ☐	105 ☐	130 ☐
6 ☐	31 ☐	56 ☐	81 ☐	106 ☐	131 ☐
7 ☐	32 ☐	57 ☐	82 ☐	107 ☐	132 ☐
8 ☐	33 ☐	58 ☐	83 ☐	108 ☐	☐
9 ☐	34 ☐	59 ☐	84 ☐	109 ☐	☐
10 ☐	35 ☐	60 ☐	85 ☐	110 ☐	☐
11 ☐	36 ☐	61 ☐	86 ☐	111 ☐	☐
12 ☐	37 ☐	62 ☐	87 ☐	112 ☐	☐
13 ☐	38 ☐	63 ☐	88 ☐	113 ☐	☐
14 ☐	39 ☐	64 ☐	89 ☐	114 ☐	☐
15 ☐	40 ☐	65 ☐	90 ☐	115 ☐	☐
16 ☐	41 ☐	66 ☐	91 ☐	116 ☐	☐
17 ☐	42 ☐	67 ☐	92 ☐	117 ☐	☐
18 ☐	43 ☐	68 ☐	93 ☐	118 ☐	☐
19 ☐	44 ☐	69 ☐	94 ☐	119 ☐	☐
20 ☐	45 ☐	70 ☐	95 ☐	120 ☐	☐
21 ☐	46 ☐	71 ☐	96 ☐	121 ☐	☐
22 ☐	47 ☐	72 ☐	97 ☐	122 ☐	☐
23 ☐	48 ☐	73 ☐	98 ☐	123 ☐	☐
24 ☐	49 ☐	74 ☐	99 ☐	124 ☐	☐
25 ☐	50 ☐	75 ☐	100 ☐	125 ☐	☐

OF CARDS I HAVE:

____

OF CARDS I NEED:

____

% OF SET FILLED:

____

KEY CARDS I HAVE: ____

____

____

____

KEY CARDS I NEED: ____

____

____

____

COMMENTS: ____

____

____

____

1960 FLEER DECALS (AFL)

KEY CARDS I HAVE:

KEY CARDS I NEED:

COMMENTS:

BOSTON PATRIOTS

OF CARDS I HAVE:

OF CARDS I NEED:

% OF SET FILLED:

8 Card Set

1960 FLEER COLLEGE PENNANT DECALS (COLLEGE)

1 2 3 4 5 6 7 8 9 10 11 12 13 14 15 16 17 18 19

KEY CARDS I HAVE:

KEY CARDS I NEED:

COMMENTS:

OF CARDS I HAVE:

OF CARDS I NEED:

% OF SET FILLED:

19 Card Set

1960 EAGLES WHITE BORDER (NFL)

KEY CARDS I HAVE:

KEY CARDS I NEED:

COMMENTS:

OF CARDS I HAVE:

OF CARDS I NEED:

% OF SET FILLED:

11 Card Set

1960 CONT. 2

1960 49ERS WHITE BORDER (NFL)

1 ☐	11 ☐	21 ☐	31 ☐	41 ☐
2 ☐	12 ☐	22 ☐	32 ☐	42 ☐
3 ☐	13 ☐	23 ☐	33 ☐	43 ☐
4 ☐	14 ☐	24 ☐	34 ☐	44 ☐
5 ☐	15 ☐	25 ☐	35 ☐	☐
6 ☐	16 ☐	26 ☐	36 ☐	☐
7 ☐	17 ☐	27 ☐	37 ☐	☐
8 ☐	18 ☐	28 ☐	38 ☐	☐
9 ☐	19 ☐	29 ☐	39 ☐	☐
10 ☐	20 ☐	30 ☐	40 ☐	☐

KEY CARDS I HAVE: ______________________ # OF CARDS I HAVE: ________

KEY CARDS I NEED: ______________________ # OF CARDS I NEED: ________

COMMENTS: ______________________ % OF SET FILLED: ________

44 Card Set

1960 GIANTS JAYS PUBLISHING (NFL)

☐	☐	☐	☐
☐	☐	☐	☐
☐	☐	☐	☐
☐	☐	☐	☐
☐	☐	☐	☐

KEY CARDS I HAVE: ______________________ # OF CARDS I HAVE: ________

KEY CARDS I NEED: ______________________ # OF CARDS I NEED: ________

COMMENTS: ______________________ % OF SET FILLED: ________

12 Card Set

1960 GIANTS SHELL / RIGER POSTERS (NFL)

1 ☐ 4 ☐ 7 ☐ 10 ☐
2 ☐ 5 ☐ 8 ☐
3 ☐ 6 ☐ 9 ☐

KEY CARDS I HAVE: ____________

KEY CARDS I NEED: ____________

COMMENTS: ____________

OF CARDS I HAVE: ____________

OF CARDS I NEED: ____________

% OF SET FILLED: ____________

10 Card Set

1960 RAMS BELL BRAND (NFL)

1 ☐ 8 ☐ 17 ☐ 25 ☐ 33 ☐
2 ☐ 10 ☐ 18 ☐ 26 ☐ 34 ☐
3 ☐ 11 ☐ 19 ☐ 27 ☐ 35 ☐
4 ☐ 12 ☐ 20 ☐ 28 ☐ 36 ☐
5 ☐ 13 ☐ 21 ☐ 29 ☐ 37 ☐
6 ☐ 14 ☐ 22 ☐ 30 ☐ 38 ☐
7 ☐ 15 ☐ 23 ☐ 31 ☐ 39 ☐
8 ☐ 16 ☐ 24 ☐ 32 ☐ ☐

FRANK RYAN
Quarterback L.A. Rams

KEY CARDS I HAVE: ____________

KEY CARDS I NEED: ____________

COMMENTS: ____________

OF CARDS I HAVE: ____________

OF CARDS I NEED: ____________

% OF SET FILLED: ____________

39 Card Set

1960 TEXANS 7-11 (AFL)

KEY CARDS I HAVE:

OF CARDS I HAVE:

KEY CARDS I NEED:

OF CARDS I NEED:

COMMENTS:

% OF SET FILLED:

11 Card Set

1960 TOPPS TEAM EMBLEM STICKERS (NFL / COLLEGE)

KEY CARDS I HAVE:

KEY CARDS I NEED:

OF CARDS I HAVE:

COMMENTS:

OF CARDS I NEED:

% OF SET FILLED:

33 Card Set

1960 TOPPS (CFL)

1 ☐	16 ☐	31 ☐	46 ☐	61 ☐	76 ☐
2 ☐	17 ☐	32 ☐	47 ☐	62 ☐	77 ☐
3 ☐	18 ☐	33 ☐	48 ☐	63 ☐	78 ☐
4 ☐	19 ☐	34 ☐	49 ☐	64 ☐	79 ☐
5 ☐	20 ☐	35 ☐	50 ☐	65 ☐	80 ☐
6 ☐	21 ☐	36 ☐	51 ☐	66 ☐	81 ☐
7 ☐	22 ☐	37 ☐	52 ☐	67 ☐	82 ☐
8 ☐	23 ☐	38 ☐	53 ☐	68 ☐	83 ☐
9 ☐	24 ☐	39 ☐	54 ☐	69 ☐	84 ☐
10 ☐	25 ☐	40 ☐	55 ☐	70 ☐	85 ☐
11 ☐	26 ☐	41 ☐	56 ☐	71 ☐	86 ☐
12 ☐	27 ☐	42 ☐	57 ☐	72 ☐	87 ☐
13 ☐	28 ☐	43 ☐	58 ☐	73 ☐	88 ☐
14 ☐	29 ☐	44 ☐	59 ☐	74 ☐	☐
15 ☐	30 ☐	45 ☐	60 ☐	75 ☐	☐

OF CARDS I HAVE: ____________

OF CARDS I NEED: ____________

% OF SET FILLED: ____________

KEY CARDS I HAVE: ____________

KEY CARDS I NEED: ____________

COMMENTS: ____________

1960 TOPPS (NFL)

1	☐	26	☐	51	☐	76	☐	101	☐	126	☐
2	☐	27	☐	52	☐	77	☐	102	☐	127	☐
3	☐	28	☐	53	☐	78	☐	103	☐	128	☐
4	☐	29	☐	54	☐	79	☐	104	☐	129	☐
5	☐	30	☐	55	☐	80	☐	105	☐	130	☐
6	☐	31	☐	56	☐	81	☐	106	☐	131	☐
7	☐	32	☐	57	☐	82	☐	107	☐	132	☐
8	☐	33	☐	58	☐	83	☐	108	☐		☐
9	☐	34	☐	59	☐	84	☐	109	☐		☐
10	☐	35	☐	60	☐	85	☐	110	☐		☐
11	☐	36	☐	61	☐	86	☐	111	☐		☐
12	☐	37	☐	62	☐	87	☐	112	☐		☐
13	☐	38	☐	63	☐	88	☐	113	☐		☐
14	☐	39	☐	64	☐	89	☐	114	☐		☐
15	☐	40	☐	65	☐	90	☐	115	☐		☐
16	☐	41	☐	66	☐	91	☐	116	☐		☐
17	☐	42	☐	67	☐	92	☐	117	☐		☐
18	☐	43	☐	68	☐	93	☐	118	☐		☐
19	☐	44	☐	69	☐	94	☐	119	☐		☐
20	☐	45	☐	70	☐	95	☐	120	☐		☐
21	☐	46	☐	71	☐	96	☐	121	☐		☐
22	☐	47	☐	72	☐	97	☐	122	☐		☐
23	☐	48	☐	73	☐	98	☐	123	☐		☐
24	☐	49	☐	74	☐	99	☐	124	☐		☐
25	☐	50	☐	75	☐	100	☐	125	☐		☐

ROOSEVELT BROWN
NEW YORK GIANTS
TACKLE

OF CARDS I HAVE: ____________

OF CARDS I NEED: ____________

% OF SET FILLED: ____________

KEY CARDS I HAVE: ____________

KEY CARDS I NEED: ____________

COMMENTS: ____________

1960-61 KAHN'S

1960 KAHN'S (NFL)

KEY CARDS I HAVE:

KEY CARDS I NEED:

COMMENTS:

OF CARDS I HAVE:

OF CARDS I NEED:

% OF SET FILLED:

38 Card Set

1961 KAHN'S (NFL)

KEY CARDS I HAVE:

KEY CARDS I NEED:

COMMENTS:

OF CARDS I HAVE:

OF CARDS I NEED:

% OF SET FILLED:

Compliments of Kahn's
"THE WIENER THE WORLD AWAITED"

36 Card Set

1960 - 61 REDSKINS

1960 REDSKINS JAYS PUBLISHING (NFL)

KEY CARDS I HAVE:

KEY CARDS I NEED:

COMMENTS:

OF CARDS I HAVE:

OF CARDS I NEED:

% OF SET FILLED:

12 Card Set

1960 - 61 REDSKINS MATCHBOOKS (NFL)

KEY CARDS I HAVE:

KEY CARDS I NEED:

COMMENTS:

OF CARDS I HAVE:

OF CARDS I NEED:

% OF SET FILLED:

20 Card Set

1961 BROWNS

1961 BROWNS CARLING BEER (NFL)

A ☐ D ☐ G ☐ L ☐
B ☐ E ☐ H ☐ ☐
C ☐ F ☐ K ☐ ☐

KEY CARDS I HAVE: ______

KEY CARDS I NEED: ______

COMMENTS: ______

OF CARDS I HAVE: ______

OF CARDS I NEED: ______

% OF SET FILLED: ______

10 Card Set

1961 BROWNS NATIONAL CITY BANK (NFL)

1 ☐	8 ☐	15 ☐	22 ☐	29 ☐	36 ☐
2 ☐	9 ☐	16 ☐	23 ☐	30 ☐	☐
3 ☐	10 ☐	17 ☐	24 ☐	31 ☐	☐
4 ☐	11 ☐	18 ☐	25 ☐	32 ☐	☐
5 ☐	12 ☐	19 ☐	26 ☐	33 ☐	☐
6 ☐	13 ☐	20 ☐	27 ☐	34 ☐	☐
7 ☐	14 ☐	21 ☐	28 ☐	35 ☐	☐

KEY CARDS I HAVE: ______

KEY CARDS I NEED: ______

COMMENTS: ______

OF CARDS I HAVE: ______

OF CARDS I NEED: ______

% OF SET FILLED: ______

36 Card Set

1961 BROWNS WHITE BORDER (NFL)

☐	☐	☐	☐	☐
☐	☐	☐	☐	☐
☐	☐	☐	☐	☐
☐	☐	☐	☐	☐
☐	☐	☐	☐	☐

KEY CARDS I HAVE: ______

KEY CARDS I NEED: ______

COMMENTS: ______

OF CARDS I HAVE: ______

OF CARDS I NEED: ______

% OF SET FILLED: ______

20 Card Set

1961

1961 CARDINALS JAYS PUBLISHING (NFL)

KEY CARDS I HAVE:

KEY CARDS I NEED:

COMMENTS:

\# OF CARDS I HAVE:

\# OF CARDS I NEED:

% OF SET FILLED:

12 Card Set

1961 COLTS JAYS PUBLISHING (NFL)

KEY CARDS I HAVE:

KEY CARDS I NEED:

COMMENTS:

\# OF CARDS I HAVE:

\# OF CARDS I NEED:

% OF SET FILLED:

12 Card Set

1961 CKNW B.C. LIONS (CFL)

1 2 3 4 5 6 7

8 9 10 11 12 13 14

15 16 17 18 19 20 21

22 23 24 25 26 27 28

29 30

KEY CARDS I HAVE:

KEY CARDS I NEED:

COMMENTS:

\# OF CARDS I HAVE:

\# OF CARDS I NEED:

% OF SET FILLED:

30 Card Set

1961 CHARGERS GOLDEN TULIP (AFL)

1 ☐ 6 ☐ 11 ☐ 16 ☐ 21 ☐
2 ☐ 7 ☐ 12 ☐ 17 ☐ 22 ☐
3 ☐ 8 ☐ 13 ☐ 18 ☐ ☐
4 ☐ 9 ☐ 14 ☐ 19 ☐ ☐
5 ☐ 10 ☐ 15 ☐ 20 ☐ ☐

KEY CARDS I HAVE: ____________________

____

KEY CARDS I NEED: ____________________

____

COMMENTS: ____________________

____

____

____

RON MIX, Charger offensive tackle from USC. Very fine tackle, team man. 6' 4", 245 lbs., 23 years old.

OF CARDS I HAVE:

____

OF CARDS I NEED:

____

% OF SET FILLED:

____

22 Card Set

1961 EAGLES JAYS PUBLISHING (NFL)

☐ ☐ ☐ ☐
☐ ☐ ☐ ☐
☐ ☐ ☐ ☐
☐ ☐ ☐ ☐
☐ ☐ ☐ ☐

KEY CARDS I HAVE: ____________________

____

KEY CARDS I NEED: ____________________

____

COMMENTS: ____________________

____

____

OF CARDS I HAVE:

____

OF CARDS I NEED:

____

% OF SET FILLED:

____

12 Card Set

NOTES

NOTES

1961 FLEER (AFL / NFL)

1	26	51	76	101	126	151	176	201
2	27	52	77	102	127	152	177	202
3	28	53	78	103	128	153	178	203
4	29	54	79	104	129	154	179	204
5	30	55	80	105	130	155	180	205
6	31	56	81	106	131	156	181	206
7	32	57	82	107	132	157	182	207
8	33	58	83	108	133	158	183	208
9	34	59	84	109	134	159	184	209
10	35	60	85	110	135	160	185	210
11	36	61	86	111	136	161	186	211
12	37	62	87	112	137	162	187	212
13	38	63	88	113	138	163	188	213
14	39	64	89	114	139	164	189	214
15	40	65	90	115	140	165	190	215
16	41	66	91	116	141	166	191	216
17	42	67	92	117	142	167	192	217
18	43	68	93	118	143	168	193	218
19	44	69	94	119	144	169	194	219
20	45	70	95	120	145	170	195	220
21	46	71	96	121	146	171	196	
22	47	72	97	122	147	172	197	
23	48	73	98	123	148	173	198	
24	49	74	99	124	149	174	199	
25	50	75	100	125	150	175	200	

JOE
SCHMIDT
LINEBACKER • DETROIT LIONS

OF CARDS I HAVE: ____________

OF CARDS I NEED: ____________

% OF SET FILLED: ____________

KEY CARDS I HAVE: ____________

KEY CARDS I NEED: ____________

COMMENTS: ____________

1961 FLEER MAGIC MESSAGE BLUE INSERTS (AFL / NFL)

1 ☐	16 ☐	31 ☐
2 ☐	17 ☐	32 ☐
3 ☐	18 ☐	33 ☐
4 ☐	19 ☐	34 ☐
5 ☐	20 ☐	35 ☐
6 ☐	21 ☐	36 ☐
7 ☐	22 ☐	37 ☐
8 ☐	23 ☐	38 ☐
9 ☐	24 ☐	39 ☐
10 ☐	25 ☐	40 ☐
11 ☐	26 ☐	☐
12 ☐	27 ☐	☐
13 ☐	28 ☐	☐
14 ☐	29 ☐	☐
15 ☐	30 ☐	☐

OF CARDS I HAVE: ________

OF CARDS I NEED: ________

% OF SET FILLED: ________

KEY CARDS I HAVE: ________

KEY CARDS I NEED: ________

COMMENTS: ________

1961 JAYS PUBLISHING

1961 GIANTS JAYS PUBLISHING (NFL)

KEY CARDS I HAVE:

KEY CARDS I NEED:

COMMENTS:

OF CARDS I HAVE:

OF CARDS I NEED:

% OF SET FILLED:

12 Card Set

1961 LIONS JAYS PUBLISHING (NFL)

KEY CARDS I HAVE:

KEY CARDS I NEED:

COMMENTS:

OF CARDS I HAVE:

OF CARDS I NEED:

% OF SET FILLED:

12 Card Set

1961 OILERS JAYS PUBLISHING (AFL)

KEY CARDS I HAVE:

KEY CARDS I NEED:

COMMENTS:

OF CARDS I HAVE:

OF CARDS I NEED:

% OF SET FILLED:

24 Card Set

1961 NU-CARD (COLLEGE)

101 ☐	116 ☐	131 ☐	146 ☐	161 ☐	176 ☐
102 ☐	117 ☐	132 ☐	147 ☐	162 ☐	177 ☐
103 ☐	118 ☐	133 ☐	148 ☐	163 ☐	178 ☐
104 ☐	119 ☐	134 ☐	149 ☐	164 ☐	179 ☐
105 ☐	120 ☐	135 ☐	150 ☐	165 ☐	180 ☐
106 ☐	121 ☐	136 ☐	151 ☐	166 ☐	☐
107 ☐	122 ☐	137 ☐	152 ☐	167 ☐	☐
108 ☐	123 ☐	138 ☐	153 ☐	168 ☐	☐
109 ☐	124 ☐	139 ☐	154 ☐	169 ☐	☐
110 ☐	125 ☐	140 ☐	155 ☐	170 ☐	☐
111 ☐	126 ☐	141 ☐	156 ☐	171 ☐	☐
112 ☐	127 ☐	142 ☐	157 ☐	172 ☐	☐
113 ☐	128 ☐	143 ☐	158 ☐	173 ☐	☐
114 ☐	129 ☐	144 ☐	159 ☐	174 ☐	☐
115 ☐	130 ☐	145 ☐	160 ☐	175 ☐	☐

TENNESSEE
MIKE LUCCI
center

OF CARDS I HAVE: ______

OF CARDS I NEED: ______

% OF SET FILLED: ______

KEY CARDS I HAVE: ______

KEY CARDS I NEED: ______

COMMENTS: ______

1961 CONT. 2

1961 PACKERS LAKE TO LAKE (NFL)

1 ☐	8 ☐	15 ☐	22 ☐	29 ☐	36 ☐
2 ☐	9 ☐	16 ☐	23 ☐	30 ☐	☐
3 ☐	10 ☐	17 ☐	24 ☐	31 ☐	☐
4 ☐	11 ☐	18 ☐	25 ☐	32 ☐	☐
5 ☐	12 ☐	19 ☐	26 ☐	33 ☐	☐
6 ☐	13 ☐	20 ☐	27 ☐	34 ☐	☐
7 ☐	14 ☐	21 ☐	28 ☐	35 ☐	☐

OF CARDS I HAVE: ____________

OF CARDS I NEED: ____________

% OF SET FILLED: ____________

KEY CARDS I HAVE: ____________

KEY CARDS I NEED: ____________

COMMENTS: ____________

36 Card Set

1961 STEELERS JAYS PUBLISHING (NFL)

☐	☐	☐	☐	☐
☐	☐	☐	☐	☐
☐	☐	☐	☐	☐

OF CARDS I HAVE: ____________

KEY CARDS I HAVE: ____________

OF CARDS I NEED: ____________

KEY CARDS I NEED: ____________

COMMENTS: ____________

% OF SET FILLED: ____________

12 Card Set

1961 TITANS JAYS PUBLISHING (AFL)

☐	☐	☐	☐	☐
☐	☐	☐	☐	☐
☐	☐	☐	☐	☐

OF CARDS I HAVE: ____________

KEY CARDS I HAVE: ____________

OF CARDS I NEED: ____________

KEY CARDS I NEED: ____________

COMMENTS: ____________

% OF SET FILLED: ____________

12 Card Set

1961 TOPPS (CFL)

1	26	51	76	101	126
2	27	52	77	102	127
3	28	53	78	103	128
4	29	54	79	104	129
5	30	55	80	105	130
6	31	56	81	106	131
7	32	57	82	107	132
8	33	58	83	108	
9	34	59	84	109	
10	35	60	85	110	
11	36	61	86	111	
12	37	62	87	112	
13	38	63	88	113	
14	39	64	89	114	
15	40	65	90	115	
16	41	66	91	116	
17	42	67	92	117	
18	43	68	93	118	
19	44	69	94	119	
20	45	70	95	120	
21	46	71	96	121	
22	47	72	97	122	
23	48	73	98	123	
24	49	74	99	124	
25	50	75	100	125	

Norm Rauhaus
Blue Bombers

OF CARDS I HAVE:

OF CARDS I NEED:

% OF SET FILLED:

KEY CARDS I HAVE:

KEY CARDS I NEED:

COMMENTS:

1961 Topps (NFL)

1	26	51	76	101	126	151	176
2	27	52	77	102	127	152	177
3	28	53	78	103	128	153	178
4	29	54	79	104	129	154	179
5	30	55	80	105	130	155	180
6	31	56	81	106	131	156	181
7	32	57	82	107	132	157	182
8	33	58	83	108	133	158	183
9	34	59	84	109	134	159	184
10	35	60	85	110	135	160	185
11	36	61	86	111	136	161	186
12	37	62	87	112	137	162	187
13	38	63	88	113	138	163	188
14	39	64	89	114	139	164	189
15	40	65	90	115	140	165	190
16	41	66	91	116	141	166	191
17	42	67	92	117	142	167	192
18	43	68	93	118	143	168	193
19	44	69	94	119	144	169	194
20	45	70	95	120	145	170	195
21	46	71	96	121	146	171	196
22	47	72	97	122	147	172	197
23	48	73	98	123	148	173	198
24	49	74	99	124	149	174	
25	50	75	100	125	150	175	

CHUCK BEDNARIK
CENTER-LINEBACKER PHILADELPHIA EAGLES

OF CARDS I HAVE:

OF CARDS I NEED:

% OF SET FILLED

KEY CARDS I HAVE:

KEY CARDS I NEED:

COMMENTS:

1961 TOPPS INSERTS

1961 TOPPS STICKERS (AFL / NFL / COLLEGE)

KEY CARDS I HAVE:

KEY CARDS I NEED:

COMMENTS:

\# OF CARDS I HAVE:

\# OF CARDS I NEED:

% OF SET FILLED:

48 Card Set

1961 TOPPS CFL TRANSFERS (CFL)

1 ☐	6 ☐	11 ☐	16 ☐	24 ☐
2 ☐	7 ☐	12 ☐	20 ☐	25 ☐
3 ☐	8 ☐	13 ☐	21 ☐	26 ☐
4 ☐	9 ☐	14 ☐	22 ☐	27 ☐
5 ☐	10 ☐	15 ☐	23 ☐	☐

KEY CARDS I HAVE:

KEY CARDS I NEED:

COMMENTS:

\# OF CARDS I HAVE:

\# OF CARDS I NEED:

% OF SET FILLED:

24 Card Set

1962

1962 CHARGERS UNION OIL (AFL)

1 2 3 4 5 6 7 8 9 10 11 12 12 13 14

KEY CARDS I HAVE:

KEY CARDS I NEED:

COMMENTS:

14 Card Set

\# OF CARDS I HAVE:

\# OF CARDS I NEED:

% OF SET FILLED:

1962 KAHNS (NFL)

Compliments of Kahn's
"THE WIENER THE WORLD AWAITED"

KEY CARDS I HAVE:

KEY CARDS I NEED:

COMMENTS:

38 Card Set

\# OF CARDS I HAVE:

\# OF CARDS I NEED:

% OF SET FILLED:

1962 CKNW B.C. LIONS (CFL)

1 2 3 4 5 6 7 8 9 10 11 12 13 14 15 16 17 18 19 20 21 22 23 24 25 26 27 28 29 30 31 32

KEY CARDS I HAVE:

KEY CARDS I NEED:

COMMENTS:

32 Card Set

\# OF CARDS I HAVE:

\# OF CARDS I NEED:

% OF SET FILLED:

1962 FLEER (AFL)

1	16	31	46	61	76
2	17	32	47	62	77
3	18	33	48	63	78
4	19	34	49	64	79
5	20	35	50	65	80
6	21	36	51	66	81
7	22	37	52	67	82
8	23	38	53	68	83
9	24	39	54	69	84
10	25	40	55	70	85
11	26	41	56	71	86
12	27	42	57	72	87
13	28	43	58	73	88
14	29	44	59	74	
15	30	45	60	75	

GEORGE BLANDA
QUARTERBACK
HOUSTON OILERS

OF CARDS I HAVE:

OF CARDS I NEED:

% OF SET FILLED:

KEY CARDS I HAVE:

KEY CARDS I NEED:

COMMENTS:

1962 POST

1962 POST CEREAL (CFL)

1 ☐	26 ☐	51 ☐	76 ☐	101 ☐	126 ☐
2 ☐	27 ☐	52 ☐	77 ☐	102 ☐	127 ☐
3 ☐	28 ☐	53 ☐	78 ☐	103 ☐	128 ☐
4 ☐	29 ☐	54 ☐	79 ☐	104 ☐	129 ☐
5 ☐	30 ☐	55 ☐	80 ☐	105 ☐	130 ☐
6 ☐	31 ☐	56 ☐	81 ☐	106 ☐	131 ☐
7 ☐	32 ☐	57 ☐	82 ☐	107 ☐	132 ☐
8 ☐	33 ☐	58 ☐	83 ☐	108 ☐	133 ☐
9 ☐	34 ☐	59 ☐	84 ☐	109 ☐	134 ☐
10 ☐	35 ☐	60 ☐	85 ☐	110 ☐	135 ☐
11 ☐	36 ☐	61 ☐	86 ☐	111 ☐	136 ☐
12 ☐	37 ☐	62 ☐	87 ☐	112 ☐	137 ☐
13 ☐	38 ☐	63 ☐	88 ☐	113 ☐	☐
14 ☐	39 ☐	64 ☐	89 ☐	114 ☐	☐
15 ☐	40 ☐	65 ☐	90 ☐	115 ☐	☐
16 ☐	41 ☐	66 ☐	91 ☐	116 ☐	☐
17 ☐	42 ☐	67 ☐	92 ☐	117 ☐	☐
18 ☐	43 ☐	68 ☐	93 ☐	118 ☐	☐
19 ☐	44 ☐	69 ☐	94 ☐	119 ☐	☐
20 ☐	45 ☐	70 ☐	95 ☐	120 ☐	☐
21 ☐	46 ☐	71 ☐	96 ☐	121 ☐	☐
22 ☐	47 ☐	72 ☐	97 ☐	122 ☐	☐
23 ☐	48 ☐	73 ☐	98 ☐	123 ☐	☐
24 ☐	49 ☐	74 ☐	99 ☐	124 ☐	☐
25 ☐	50 ☐	75 ☐	100 ☐	125 ☐	☐

OF CARDS I HAVE: ____________

OF CARDS I NEED: ____________

% OF SET FILLED: ____________

KEY CARDS I HAVE: ____________

KEY CARDS I NEED: ____________

COMMENTS: ____________

137 Card Set

1962 POST BOOKLETS (NFL)

1 ☐ 2 ☐ 3 ☐ 4 ☐ ☐

KEY CARDS I HAVE: ____________

KEY CARDS I NEED: ____________

COMMENTS: ____________

OF CARDS I HAVE: ____________

OF CARDS I NEED: ____________

% OF SET FILLED: ____________

4 Card Set

1962 POST CEREAL (NFL)

141

Bob Lilly

DALLAS COWBOYS END

Ht. 6'4"; Wt. 250; Born July 26, 1939
College ... Texas Christian University
Home .... Throckmorton, Texas

The Cowboys' No. 1 draft choice in 1961, Bob was an All-Southwest Conference tackle in 1959 and '60. He was also everyone's All-American at TCU in 1960. Extremely strong and agile, he proved to be one of the top rookies in the National Football League in 1961. NFL coaches agree that with experience he will be one of the outstanding defensive linemen in NFL history.

Post

1	☐	26	☐	51	☐	76	☐	101	☐	126	☐	151	☐	176	☐
2	☐	27	☐	52	☐	77	☐	102	☐	127	☐	152	☐	177	☐
3	☐	28	☐	53	☐	78	☐	103	☐	128	☐	153	☐	178	☐
4	☐	29	☐	54	☐	79	☐	104	☐	129	☐	154	☐	179	☐
5	☐	30	☐	55	☐	80	☐	105	☐	130	☐	155	☐	180	☐
6	☐	31	☐	56	☐	81	☐	106	☐	131	☐	156	☐	181	☐
7	☐	32	☐	57	☐	82	☐	107	☐	132	☐	157	☐	182	☐
8	☐	33	☐	58	☐	83	☐	108	☐	133	☐	158	☐	183	☐
9	☐	34	☐	59	☐	84	☐	109	☐	134	☐	159	☐	184	☐
10	☐	35	☐	60	☐	85	☐	110	☐	135	☐	160	☐	185	☐
11	☐	36	☐	61	☐	86	☐	111	☐	136	☐	161	☐	186	☐
12	☐	37	☐	62	☐	87	☐	112	☐	137	☐	162	☐	187	☐
13	☐	38	☐	63	☐	88	☐	113	☐	138	☐	163	☐	188	☐
14	☐	39	☐	64	☐	89	☐	114	☐	139	☐	164	☐	189	☐
15	☐	40	☐	65	☐	90	☐	115	☐	140	☐	165	☐	190	☐
16	☐	41	☐	66	☐	91	☐	116	☐	141	☐	166	☐	191	☐
17	☐	42	☐	67	☐	92	☐	117	☐	142	☐	167	☐	192	☐
18	☐	43	☐	68	☐	93	☐	118	☐	143	☐	168	☐	193	☐
19	☐	44	☐	69	☐	94	☐	119	☐	144	☐	169	☐	194	☐
20	☐	45	☐	70	☐	95	☐	120	☐	145	☐	170	☐	195	☐
21	☐	46	☐	71	☐	96	☐	121	☐	146	☐	171	☐	196	☐
22	☐	47	☐	72	☐	97	☐	122	☐	147	☐	172	☐	197	☐
23	☐	48	☐	73	☐	98	☐	123	☐	148	☐	173	☐	198	☐
24	☐	49	☐	74	☐	99	☐	124	☐	149	☐	174	☐	199	☐
25	☐	50	☐	75	☐	100	☐	125	☐	150	☐	175	☐	200	☐

OF CARDS I HAVE: ____________

OF CARDS I NEED: ____________

% OF SET FILLED: ____________

KEY CARDS I HAVE:

KEY CARDS I NEED:

COMMENTS:

1962 SALADA COINS (NFL)

1	26	51	76	101	126	151
2	27	52	77	102	127	152
3	28	53	78	103	128	153
4	29	54	79	104	129	154
5	30	55	80	105	130	
6	31	56	81	106	131	
7	32	57	82	107	132	
8	33	58	83	108	133	
9	34	59	84	109	134	
10	35	60	85	110	135	
11	36	61	86	111	136	
12	37	62	87	112	137	
13	38	63	88	113	138	
14	39	64	89	114	139	
15	40	65	90	115	140	
16	41	66	91	116	141	
17	42	67	92	117	142	
18	43	68	93	118	143	
19	44	69	94	119	144	
20	45	70	95	120	145	
21	46	71	96	121	146	
22	47	72	97	122	147	
23	48	73	98	123	148	
24	49	74	99	124	149	
25	50	75	100	125	150	

OF CARDS I HAVE: ________

OF CARDS I NEED: ________

% OF SET FILLED: ________

KEY CARDS I HAVE:

KEY CARDS I NEED:

COMMENTS:

1962 TOPPS (CFL)

1	26	51	76	101	126	151
2	27	52	77	102	127	152
3	28	53	78	103	128	153
4	29	54	79	104	129	154
5	30	55	80	105	130	155
6	31	56	81	106	131	156
7	32	57	82	107	132	157
8	33	58	83	108	133	158
9	34	59	84	109	134	159
10	35	60	85	110	135	160
11	36	61	86	111	136	161
12	37	62	87	112	137	162
13	38	63	88	113	138	163
14	39	64	89	114	139	164
15	40	65	90	115	140	165
16	41	66	91	116	141	166
17	42	67	92	117	142	167
18	43	68	93	118	143	168
19	44	69	94	119	144	169
20	45	70	95	120	145	
21	46	71	96	121	146	
22	47	72	97	122	147	
23	48	73	98	123	148	
24	49	74	99	124	149	
25	50	75	100	125	150	

JOE CARRUTHERS
CALGARY STAMPEDERS

OF CARDS I HAVE: ________

OF CARDS I NEED: ________

% OF SET FILLED: ________

KEY CARDS I HAVE: ________

KEY CARDS I NEED: ________

COMMENTS: ________

1962 Topps (NFL)

1	26	51	76	101	126	151	
2	27	52	77	102	127	152	
3	28	53	78	103	128	153	
4	29	54	79	104	129	154	
5	30	55	80	105	130	155	
6	31	56	81	106	131	156	
7	32	57	82	107	132	157	
8	33	58	83	108	133	158	
9	34	59	84	109	134	159	
10	35	60	85	110	135	160	
11	36	61	86	111	136	161	176
12	37	62	87	112	137	162	
13	38	63	88	113	138	163	
14	39	64	89	114	139	164	
15	40	65	90	115	140	165	
16	41	66	91	116	141	166	
17	42	67	92	117	142	167	
18	43	68	93	118	143	168	
19	44	69	94	119	144	169	
20	45	70	95	120	145	170	
21	46	71	96	121	146	171	
22	47	72	97	122	147	172	
23	48	73	98	123	148	173	
24	49	74	99	124	149	174	
25	50	75	100	125	150	175	

ALEX
KARRAS
DETROIT LIONS
DEFENS. TACKLE

OF CARDS I HAVE: ____________

OF CARDS I NEED: ____________

% OF SET FILLED: ____________

KEY CARDS I HAVE:

KEY CARDS I NEED:

COMMENTS:

1962 TANG TEAM PHOTOS (NFL)

1 ☐	5 ☐	9 ☐	13 ☐	☐
2 ☐	6 ☐	10 ☐	14 ☐	☐
3 ☐	7 ☐	11 ☐	☐	☐
4 ☐	8 ☐	12 ☐	☐	☐

KEY CARDS I HAVE: ______________________

OF CARDS I HAVE: ______________

KEY CARDS I NEED: ______________________

OF CARDS I NEED: ______________

COMMENTS: ______________________

% OF SET FILLED: ______________

14 Card Set

1962 TOPPS BUCKS (NFL)

1 ☐	11 ☐	21 ☐	31 ☐	41 ☐
2 ☐	12 ☐	22 ☐	32 ☐	42 ☐
3 ☐	13 ☐	23 ☐	33 ☐	43 ☐
4 ☐	14 ☐	24 ☐	34 ☐	44 ☐
5 ☐	15 ☐	25 ☐	35 ☐	45 ☐
6 ☐	16 ☐	26 ☐	36 ☐	46 ☐
7 ☐	17 ☐	27 ☐	37 ☐	47 ☐
8 ☐	18 ☐	28 ☐	38 ☐	48 ☐
9 ☐	19 ☐	29 ☐	39 ☐	☐
10 ☐	20 ☐	30 ☐	40 ☐	☐

OF CARDS I HAVE: ______________

KEY CARDS I HAVE: ______________________

OF CARDS I NEED: ______________

KEY CARDS I NEED: ______________________

% OF SET FILLED: ______________

COMMENTS: ______________________

48 Card Set

1963

1963 BILLS JONES DIARY (AFL)

KEY CARDS I HAVE:

OF CARDS I HAVE:

KEY CARDS I NEED:

OF CARDS I NEED:

COMMENTS:

% OF SET FILLED:

40 Card Set

1963 BROWNS WHITE BORDER (NFL)

KEY CARDS I HAVE:

OF CARDS I HAVE:

KEY CARDS I NEED:

OF CARDS I NEED:

COMMENTS:

% OF SET FILLED:

26 Card Set

1963 FLEER (AFL)

1 ☐	16 ☐	31 ☐	46 ☐	61 ☐	76 ☐
2 ☐	17 ☐	32 ☐	47 ☐	62 ☐	77 ☐
3 ☐	18 ☐	33 ☐	48 ☐	63 ☐	78 ☐
4 ☐	19 ☐	34 ☐	49 ☐	64 ☐	79 ☐
5 ☐	20 ☐	35 ☐	50 ☐	65 ☐	80 ☐
6 ☐	21 ☐	36 ☐	51 ☐	66 ☐	81 ☐
7 ☐	22 ☐	37 ☐	52 ☐	67 ☐	82 ☐
8 ☐	23 ☐	38 ☐	53 ☐	68 ☐	83 ☐
9 ☐	24 ☐	39 ☐	54 ☐	69 ☐	84 ☐
10 ☐	25 ☐	40 ☐	55 ☐	70 ☐	85 ☐
11 ☐	26 ☐	41 ☐	56 ☐	71 ☐	86 ☐
12 ☐	27 ☐	42 ☐	57 ☐	72 ☐	87 ☐
13 ☐	28 ☐	43 ☐	58 ☐	73 ☐	88 ☐
14 ☐	29 ☐	44 ☐	59 ☐	74 ☐	☐
15 ☐	30 ☐	45 ☐	60 ☐	75 ☐	☐

JIM OTTO
CENTER
OAKLAND RAIDERS

OF CARDS I HAVE: ____________

OF CARDS I NEED: ____________

% OF SET FILLED: ____________

KEY CARDS I HAVE: ____________________

KEY CARDS I NEED: ____________________

COMMENTS: ____________________

1963 KAHN'S (NFL)

Compliments of Kahn's
"THE WIENER THE WORLD AWAITED"

OF CARDS I HAVE:

OF CARDS I NEED:

% OF SET FILLED:

KEY CARDS I HAVE:

KEY CARDS I NEED:

COMMENTS:

1963 NALLEY'S COINS (CFL)

1	26	51	76	101	126	151
2	27	52	77	102	127	152
3	28	53	78	103	128	153
4	29	54	79	104	129	154
5	30	55	80	105	130	155
6	31	56	81	106	131	156
7	32	57	82	107	132	157
8	33	58	83	108	133	158
9	34	59	84	109	134	159
10	35	60	85	110	135	160
11	36	61	86	111	136	
12	37	62	87	112	137	
13	38	63	88	113	138	
14	39	64	89	114	139	
15	40	65	90	115	140	
16	41	66	91	116	141	
17	42	67	92	117	142	
18	43	68	93	118	143	
19	44	69	94	119	144	
20	45	70	95	120	145	
21	46	71	96	121	146	
22	47	72	97	122	147	
23	48	73	98	123	148	
24	49	74	99	124	149	
25	50	75	100	125	150	

OF CARDS I HAVE: ______

OF CARDS I NEED: ______

% OF SET FILLED: ______

KEY CARDS I HAVE: ______

KEY CARDS I NEED: ______

COMMENTS: ______

1963 POST CEREAL (CFL)

Bill Crawford 110
Guard - CALGARY STAMPEDERS - Garde
Ht. 6-1; Wt. 230; Age 26
Home - Vancouver, B.C. Univ. of B.C.
Taille 6-1; Poids 230; Age 26
Résidence - Van. Univ. de la Colombie-Britannique

1 ☐	26 ☐	51 ☐	76 ☐	101 ☐	126 ☐	151 ☐
2 ☐	27 ☐	52 ☐	77 ☐	102 ☐	127 ☐	152 ☐
3 ☐	28 ☐	53 ☐	78 ☐	103 ☐	128 ☐	153 ☐
4 ☐	29 ☐	54 ☐	79 ☐	104 ☐	129 ☐	154 ☐
5 ☐	30 ☐	55 ☐	80 ☐	105 ☐	130 ☐	155 ☐
6 ☐	31 ☐	56 ☐	81 ☐	106 ☐	131 ☐	156 ☐
7 ☐	32 ☐	57 ☐	82 ☐	107 ☐	132 ☐	157 ☐
8 ☐	33 ☐	58 ☐	83 ☐	108 ☐	133 ☐	158 ☐
9 ☐	34 ☐	59 ☐	84 ☐	109 ☐	134 ☐	159 ☐
10 ☐	35 ☐	60 ☐	85 ☐	110 ☐	135 ☐	160 ☐
11 ☐	36 ☐	61 ☐	86 ☐	111 ☐	136 ☐	
12 ☐	37 ☐	62 ☐	87 ☐	112 ☐	137 ☐	
13 ☐	38 ☐	63 ☐	88 ☐	113 ☐	138 ☐	
14 ☐	39 ☐	64 ☐	89 ☐	114 ☐	139 ☐	
15 ☐	40 ☐	65 ☐	90 ☐	115 ☐	140 ☐	
16 ☐	41 ☐	66 ☐	91 ☐	116 ☐	141 ☐	
17 ☐	42 ☐	67 ☐	92 ☐	117 ☐	142 ☐	
18 ☐	43 ☐	68 ☐	93 ☐	118 ☐	143 ☐	
19 ☐	44 ☐	69 ☐	94 ☐	119 ☐	144 ☐	
20 ☐	45 ☐	70 ☐	95 ☐	120 ☐	145 ☐	
21 ☐	46 ☐	71 ☐	96 ☐	121 ☐	146 ☐	
22 ☐	47 ☐	72 ☐	97 ☐	122 ☐	147 ☐	
23 ☐	48 ☐	73 ☐	98 ☐	123 ☐	148 ☐	
24 ☐	49 ☐	74 ☐	99 ☐	124 ☐	149 ☐	
25 ☐	50 ☐	75 ☐	100 ☐	125 ☐	150 ☐	

OF CARDS I HAVE: ____________

OF CARDS I NEED: ____________

% OF SET FILLED: ____________

KEY CARDS I HAVE: ____________________

KEY CARDS I NEED: ____________________

COMMENTS: ____________________

1963 STANCRAFT PLAYING CARDS (NFL)

1 ☐	11 ☐	21 ☐	31 ☐	41 ☐	51 ☐
2 ☐	12 ☐	22 ☐	32 ☐	42 ☐	52 ☐
3 ☐	13 ☐	23 ☐	33 ☐	43 ☐	53 ☐
4 ☐	14 ☐	24 ☐	34 ☐	44 ☐	54 ☐
5 ☐	15 ☐	25 ☐	35 ☐	45 ☐	☐
6 ☐	16 ☐	26 ☐	36 ☐	46 ☐	☐
7 ☐	17 ☐	27 ☐	37 ☐	47 ☐	☐
8 ☐	18 ☐	28 ☐	38 ☐	48 ☐	☐
9 ☐	19 ☐	29 ☐	39 ☐	49 ☐	☐
10 ☐	20 ☐	30 ☐	40 ☐	50 ☐	☐

KEY CARDS I HAVE: ______________________

OF CARDS I HAVE: ______________

KEY CARDS I NEED: ______________________

OF CARDS I NEED: ______________

COMMENTS: ______________________

% OF SET FILLED: ______________

54 Card Set

1963 STEELERS IDL (NFL)

☐	☐	☐	☐	☐	☐
☐	☐	☐	☐	☐	☐
☐	☐	☐	☐	☐	☐
☐	☐	☐	☐	☐	☐
☐	☐	☐	☐	☐	☐

KEY CARDS I HAVE: ______________________

OF CARDS I HAVE: ______________

KEY CARDS I NEED: ______________________

OF CARDS I NEED: ______________

COMMENTS: ______________________

% OF SET FILLED: ______________

26 Card Set

1963 TOPPS (NFL)

1 ☐	26 ☐	51 ☐	76 ☐	101 ☐	126 ☐	151 ☐
2 ☐	27 ☐	52 ☐	77 ☐	102 ☐	127 ☐	152 ☐
3 ☐	28 ☐	53 ☐	78 ☐	103 ☐	128 ☐	153 ☐
4 ☐	29 ☐	54 ☐	79 ☐	104 ☐	129 ☐	154 ☐
5 ☐	30 ☐	55 ☐	80 ☐	105 ☐	130 ☐	155 ☐
6 ☐	31 ☐	56 ☐	81 ☐	106 ☐	131 ☐	156 ☐
7 ☐	32 ☐	57 ☐	82 ☐	107 ☐	132 ☐	157 ☐
8 ☐	33 ☐	58 ☐	83 ☐	108 ☐	133 ☐	158 ☐
9 ☐	34 ☐	59 ☐	84 ☐	109 ☐	134 ☐	159 ☐
10 ☐	35 ☐	60 ☐	85 ☐	110 ☐	135 ☐	160 ☐
11 ☐	36 ☐	61 ☐	86 ☐	111 ☐	136 ☐	161 ☐
12 ☐	37 ☐	62 ☐	87 ☐	112 ☐	137 ☐	162 ☐
13 ☐	38 ☐	63 ☐	88 ☐	113 ☐	138 ☐	163 ☐
14 ☐	39 ☐	64 ☐	89 ☐	114 ☐	139 ☐	164 ☐
15 ☐	40 ☐	65 ☐	90 ☐	115 ☐	140 ☐	165 ☐
16 ☐	41 ☐	66 ☐	91 ☐	116 ☐	141 ☐	166 ☐
17 ☐	42 ☐	67 ☐	92 ☐	117 ☐	142 ☐	167 ☐
18 ☐	43 ☐	68 ☐	93 ☐	118 ☐	143 ☐	168 ☐
19 ☐	44 ☐	69 ☐	94 ☐	119 ☐	144 ☐	169 ☐
20 ☐	45 ☐	70 ☐	95 ☐	120 ☐	145 ☐	170 ☐
21 ☐	46 ☐	71 ☐	96 ☐	121 ☐	146 ☐	☐
22 ☐	47 ☐	72 ☐	97 ☐	122 ☐	147 ☐	☐
23 ☐	48 ☐	73 ☐	98 ☐	123 ☐	148 ☐	☐
24 ☐	49 ☐	74 ☐	99 ☐	124 ☐	149 ☐	☐
25 ☐	50 ☐	75 ☐	100 ☐	125 ☐	150 ☐	☐

OF CARDS I HAVE: ____________

OF CARDS I NEED: ____________

% OF SET FILLED: ____________

KEY CARDS I HAVE: ____

KEY CARDS I NEED: ____

COMMENTS: ____

1963 TOPPS (CFL)

1 ☐	16 ☐	31 ☐	46 ☐	61 ☐	76 ☐
2 ☐	17 ☐	32 ☐	47 ☐	62 ☐	77 ☐
3 ☐	18 ☐	33 ☐	48 ☐	63 ☐	78 ☐
4 ☐	19 ☐	34 ☐	49 ☐	64 ☐	79 ☐
5 ☐	20 ☐	35 ☐	50 ☐	65 ☐	80 ☐
6 ☐	21 ☐	36 ☐	51 ☐	66 ☐	81 ☐
7 ☐	22 ☐	37 ☐	52 ☐	67 ☐	82 ☐
8 ☐	23 ☐	38 ☐	53 ☐	68 ☐	83 ☐
9 ☐	24 ☐	39 ☐	54 ☐	69 ☐	84 ☐
10 ☐	25 ☐	40 ☐	55 ☐	70 ☐	85 ☐
11 ☐	26 ☐	41 ☐	56 ☐	71 ☐	86 ☐
12 ☐	27 ☐	42 ☐	57 ☐	72 ☐	87 ☐
13 ☐	28 ☐	43 ☐	58 ☐	73 ☐	88 ☐
14 ☐	29 ☐	44 ☐	59 ☐	74 ☐	☐
15 ☐	30 ☐	45 ☐	60 ☐	75 ☐	☐

ED BUCHANAN CALGARY STAMPEDERS

OF CARDS I HAVE: ____________

OF CARDS I NEED: ____________

% OF SET FILLED: ____________

KEY CARDS I HAVE: ____________

KEY CARDS I NEED: ____________

COMMENTS: ____________

1964 NALLEY'S COINS (CFL)

1 ☐	16 ☐	31 ☐	46 ☐	61 ☐	76 ☐	91 ☐
2 ☐	17 ☐	32 ☐	47 ☐	62 ☐	77 ☐	92 ☐
3 ☐	18 ☐	33 ☐	48 ☐	63 ☐	78 ☐	93 ☐
4 ☐	19 ☐	34 ☐	49 ☐	64 ☐	79 ☐	94 ☐
5 ☐	20 ☐	35 ☐	50 ☐	65 ☐	80 ☐	95 ☐
6 ☐	21 ☐	36 ☐	51 ☐	66 ☐	81 ☐	96 ☐
7 ☐	22 ☐	37 ☐	52 ☐	67 ☐	82 ☐	97 ☐
8 ☐	23 ☐	38 ☐	53 ☐	68 ☐	83 ☐	98 ☐
9 ☐	24 ☐	39 ☐	54 ☐	69 ☐	84 ☐	99 ☐
10 ☐	25 ☐	40 ☐	55 ☐	70 ☐	85 ☐	100 ☐
11 ☐	26 ☐	41 ☐	56 ☐	71 ☐	86 ☐	☐
12 ☐	27 ☐	42 ☐	57 ☐	72 ☐	87 ☐	☐
13 ☐	28 ☐	43 ☐	58 ☐	73 ☐	88 ☐	☐
14 ☐	29 ☐	44 ☐	59 ☐	74 ☐	89 ☐	☐
15 ☐	30 ☐	45 ☐	60 ☐	75 ☐	90 ☐	☐

OF CARDS I HAVE: ____________

OF CARDS I NEED: ____________

% OF SET FILLED: ____________

KEY CARDS I HAVE: ______________________________

KEY CARDS I NEED: ______________________________

COMMENTS: ______________________________

1964 PHILADELPHIA (NFL)

1	26	51	76	101	126	151	176
2	27	52	77	102	127	152	177
3	28	53	78	103	128	153	178
4	29	54	79	104	129	154	179
5	30	55	80	105	130	155	180
6	31	56	81	106	131	156	181
7	32	57	82	107	132	157	182
8	33	58	83	108	133	158	183
9	34	59	84	109	134	159	184
10	35	60	85	110	135	160	185
11	36	61	86	111	136	161	186
12	37	62	87	112	137	162	187
13	38	63	88	113	138	163	188
14	39	64	89	114	139	164	189
15	40	65	90	115	140	165	190
16	41	66	91	116	141	166	191
17	42	67	92	117	142	167	192
18	43	68	93	118	143	168	193
19	44	69	94	119	144	169	194
20	45	70	95	120	145	170	195
21	46	71	96	121	146	171	196
22	47	72	97	122	147	172	197
23	48	73	98	123	148	173	198
24	49	74	99	124	149	174	
25	50	75	100	125	150	175	

OF CARDS I HAVE: ____________

OF CARDS I NEED: ____________

% OF SET FILLED: ____________

KEY CARDS I HAVE: ____________

KEY CARDS I NEED: ____________

COMMENTS: ____________

1964 Topps (AFL)

1	26	51	76	101	126	151	
2	27	52	77	102	127	152	
3	28	53	78	103	128	153	
4	29	54	79	104	129	154	
5	30	55	80	105	130	155	
6	31	56	81	106	131	156	
7	32	57	82	107	132	157	
8	33	58	83	108	133	158	
9	34	59	84	109	134	159	
10	35	60	85	110	135	160	
11	36	61	86	111	136	161	
12	37	62	87	112	137	162	
13	38	63	88	113	138	163	
14	39	64	89	114	139	164	
15	40	65	90	115	140	165	176
16	41	66	91	116	141	166	
17	42	67	92	117	142	167	
18	43	68	93	118	143	168	
19	44	69	94	119	144	169	
20	45	70	95	120	145	170	
21	46	71	96	121	146	171	
22	47	72	97	122	147	172	
23	48	73	98	123	148	173	
24	49	74	99	124	149	174	
25	50	75	100	125	150	175	

JACK KEMP
BUFFALO BILLS QUARTERBACK

OF CARDS I HAVE: ____________

OF CARDS I NEED: ____________

% OF SET FILLED: ____________

KEY CARDS I HAVE: ____________

KEY CARDS I NEED: ____________

COMMENTS: ____________

1964 TOPPS (CFL)

1 ☐	16 ☐	31 ☐	46 ☐	61 ☐	76 ☐
2 ☐	17 ☐	32 ☐	47 ☐	62 ☐	77 ☐
3 ☐	18 ☐	33 ☐	48 ☐	63 ☐	78 ☐
4 ☐	19 ☐	34 ☐	49 ☐	64 ☐	79 ☐
5 ☐	20 ☐	35 ☐	50 ☐	65 ☐	80 ☐
6 ☐	21 ☐	36 ☐	51 ☐	66 ☐	81 ☐
7 ☐	22 ☐	37 ☐	52 ☐	67 ☐	82 ☐
8 ☐	23 ☐	38 ☐	53 ☐	68 ☐	83 ☐
9 ☐	24 ☐	39 ☐	54 ☐	69 ☐	84 ☐
10 ☐	25 ☐	40 ☐	55 ☐	70 ☐	85 ☐
11 ☐	26 ☐	41 ☐	56 ☐	71 ☐	86 ☐
12 ☐	27 ☐	42 ☐	57 ☐	72 ☐	87 ☐
13 ☐	28 ☐	43 ☐	58 ☐	73 ☐	88 ☐
14 ☐	29 ☐	44 ☐	59 ☐	74 ☐	☐
15 ☐	30 ☐	45 ☐	60 ☐	75 ☐	☐

CALGARY
STAMPEDERS
JERRY KEELING
QUARTERBACK

\# OF CARDS I HAVE: ____________

\# OF CARDS I NEED: ____________

% OF SET FILLED: ____________

KEY CARDS I HAVE:

KEY CARDS I NEED:

COMMENTS:

1964

1964 TOPPS PENNANT STICKERS (AFL / COLLEGE)

KEY CARDS I HAVE:

\# OF CARDS I HAVE:

KEY CARDS I NEED:

\# OF CARDS I NEED:

COMMENTS:

% OF SET FILLED:

24 Card Set

1964 WHEATIES STAMPS (NFL)

KEY CARDS I HAVE:

\# OF CARDS I HAVE:

KEY CARDS I NEED:

\# OF CARDS I NEED:

COMMENTS:

% OF SET FILLED:

74 Card Set

1964 - 65

1964 KAHN'S (NFL)

OF CARDS I HAVE:

OF CARDS I NEED:

% OF SET FILLED:

KEY CARDS I HAVE:

KEY CARDS I NEED:

COMMENTS:

53 Card Set

1964-65 OILERS COLOR TEAM (AFL)

KEY CARDS I HAVE:

OF CARDS I HAVE:

KEY CARDS I NEED:

OF CARDS I NEED:

COMMENTS:

% OF SET FILLED:

16 Card Set

NOTES

NOTES

1964 - 69

1964 - 69 CHIEFS FAIRMONT DAIRY (AFL)

1 ☐ 6 ☐ 11 ☐ 16 ☐ ☐
2 ☐ 7 ☐ 12 ☐ 17 ☐ ☐
3 ☐ 8 ☐ 13 ☐ 18 ☐ ☐
4 ☐ 9 ☐ 14 ☐ 19 ☐ ☐
5 ☐ 10 ☐ 15 ☐ ☐ ☐

KEY CARDS I HAVE: # OF CARDS I HAVE:

KEY CARDS I NEED: # OF CARDS I NEED:

COMMENTS: % OF SET FILLED:

19 Card Set

1964 LIONS WHITE BORDER (NFL)

☐ ☐ ☐ ☐ ☐
☐ ☐ ☐ ☐ ☐
☐ ☐ ☐ ☐ ☐
☐ ☐ ☐ ☐ ☐
☐ ☐ ☐ ☐ ☐
☐ ☐ ☐ ☐ ☐

KEY CARDS I HAVE: # OF CARDS I HAVE:

KEY CARDS I NEED: # OF CARDS I NEED:

COMMENTS: % OF SET FILLED:

24 Card Set

1965

1965 BILLS SUPER DUPER MARKETS (AFL)

OF CARDS I HAVE:

OF CARDS I NEED:

KEY CARDS I HAVE:

KEY CARDS I NEED:

% OF SET FILLED:

COMMENTS:

10 Card Set

1965 CARDINALS BIG RED BIOGRAPHIES (NFL)

OF CARDS I HAVE:

OF CARDS I NEED:

KEY CARDS I HAVE:

KEY CARDS I NEED:

% OF SET FILLED:

COMMENTS:

17 Card Set

1965 CARDINALS TEAM ISSUE (NFL)

OF CARDS I HAVE:

OF CARDS I NEED:

KEY CARDS I HAVE:

KEY CARDS I NEED:

% OF SET FILLED:

COMMENTS:

10 Card Set

1965 PHILADELPHIA (NFL)

1	26	51	76	101	126	151	176
2	27	52	77	102	127	152	177
3	28	53	78	103	128	153	178
4	29	54	79	104	129	154	179
5	30	55	80	105	130	155	180
6	31	56	81	106	131	156	181
7	32	57	82	107	132	157	182
8	33	58	83	108	133	158	183
9	34	59	84	109	134	159	184
10	35	60	85	110	135	160	185
11	36	61	86	111	136	161	186
12	37	62	87	112	137	162	187
13	38	63	88	113	138	163	188
14	39	64	89	114	139	164	189
15	40	65	90	115	140	165	190
16	41	66	91	116	141	166	191
17	42	67	92	117	142	167	192
18	43	68	93	118	143	168	193
19	44	69	94	119	144	169	194
20	45	70	95	120	145	170	195
21	46	71	96	121	146	171	196
22	47	72	97	122	147	172	197
23	48	73	98	123	148	173	198
24	49	74	99	124	149	174	
25	50	75	100	125	150	175	

OF CARDS I HAVE:

OF CARDS I NEED:

% OF SET FILLED

KEY CARDS I HAVE:

KEY CARDS I NEED:

COMMENTS:

1965 TOPPS (CFL)

TACKLE / OTTAWA ROUGHRIDERS
BILL SIEKIERSKI

1 ☐	26 ☐	51 ☐	76 ☐	101 ☐	126 ☐
2 ☐	27 ☐	52 ☐	77 ☐	102 ☐	127 ☐
3 ☐	28 ☐	53 ☐	78 ☐	103 ☐	128 ☐
4 ☐	29 ☐	54 ☐	79 ☐	104 ☐	129 ☐
5 ☐	30 ☐	55 ☐	80 ☐	105 ☐	130 ☐
6 ☐	31 ☐	56 ☐	81 ☐	106 ☐	131 ☐
7 ☐	32 ☐	57 ☐	82 ☐	107 ☐	132 ☐
8 ☐	33 ☐	58 ☐	83 ☐	108 ☐	☐
9 ☐	34 ☐	59 ☐	84 ☐	109 ☐	☐
10 ☐	35 ☐	60 ☐	85 ☐	110 ☐	☐
11 ☐	36 ☐	61 ☐	86 ☐	111 ☐	☐
12 ☐	37 ☐	62 ☐	87 ☐	112 ☐	☐
13 ☐	38 ☐	63 ☐	88 ☐	113 ☐	☐
14 ☐	39 ☐	64 ☐	89 ☐	114 ☐	☐
15 ☐	40 ☐	65 ☐	90 ☐	115 ☐	☐
16 ☐	41 ☐	66 ☐	91 ☐	116 ☐	☐
17 ☐	42 ☐	67 ☐	92 ☐	117 ☐	☐
18 ☐	43 ☐	68 ☐	93 ☐	118 ☐	☐
19 ☐	44 ☐	69 ☐	94 ☐	119 ☐	☐
20 ☐	45 ☐	70 ☐	95 ☐	120 ☐	☐
21 ☐	46 ☐	71 ☐	96 ☐	121 ☐	☐
22 ☐	47 ☐	72 ☐	97 ☐	122 ☐	☐
23 ☐	48 ☐	73 ☐	98 ☐	123 ☐	☐
24 ☐	49 ☐	74 ☐	99 ☐	124 ☐	☐
25 ☐	50 ☐	75 ☐	100 ☐	125 ☐	☐

OF CARDS I HAVE: ____________

OF CARDS I NEED: ____________

% OF SET FILLED: ____________

KEY CARDS I HAVE: ____________

KEY CARDS I NEED: ____________

COMMENTS: ____________

1965 TOPPS INSERTS

1965 TOPPS RUB-OFFS (AFL / COLLEGE)

KEY CARDS I HAVE:

KEY CARDS I NEED:

COMMENTS:

OF CARDS I HAVE:

OF CARDS I NEED:

% OF SET FILLED:

36 Card Set

1965 TOPPS CFL TRANSFERS (CFL)

1	6	11	16	21	26
2	7	12	17	22	27
3	8	13	18	23	
4	9	14	19	24	
5	10	15	20	25	

KEY CARDS I HAVE:

KEY CARDS I NEED:

COMMENTS:

OF CARDS I HAVE:

OF CARDS I NEED:

% OF SET FILLED:

27 Card Set

1965 Topps (AFL)

1	26	51	76	101	126	151	
2	27	52	77	102	127	152	
3	28	53	78	103	128	153	
4	29	54	79	104	129	154	
5	30	55	80	105	130	155	
6	31	56	81	106	131	156	
7	32	57	82	107	132	157	
8	33	58	83	108	133	158	
9	34	59	84	109	134	159	
10	35	60	85	110	135	160	
11	36	61	86	111	136	161	
12	37	62	87	112	137	162	
13	38	63	88	113	138	163	
14	39	64	89	114	139	164	
15	40	65	90	115	140	165	176
16	41	66	91	116	141	166	
17	42	67	92	117	142	167	
18	43	68	93	118	143	168	
19	44	69	94	119	144	169	
20	45	70	95	120	145	170	
21	46	71	96	121	146	171	
22	47	72	97	122	147	172	
23	48	73	98	123	148	173	
24	49	74	99	124	149	174	
25	50	75	100	125	150	175	

NEW YORK

JOE NAMATH quarterback

OF CARDS I HAVE: ______

OF CARDS I NEED: ______

% OF SET FILLED: ______

KEY CARDS I HAVE:

KEY CARDS I NEED:

COMMENTS:

1966

1966 AMERICAN OIL ALL-PRO (NFL)

1 ☐ 2 ☐ 3 ☐ 4 ☐ 5 ☐ 6 ☐ 7 ☐ 8 ☐ 9 ☐ 10 ☐ 11 ☐ 12 ☐ 13 ☐ 14 ☐ 15 ☐ 16 ☐ 17 ☐ 18 ☐ 19 ☐ 20 ☐ ☐ ☐ ☐ ☐

Bob Lilly
COWBOYS

KEY CARDS I HAVE: ____________________

KEY CARDS I NEED: ____________________

COMMENTS: ____________________

OF CARDS I HAVE: ____________

OF CARDS I NEED: ____________

% OF SET FILLED: ____________

15 Card Set

1966 CHARGERS WHITE BORDER (AFL)

1 ☐ 2 ☐ 3 ☐ 4 ☐ 5 ☐ 6 ☐ 7 ☐ 8 ☐ 9 ☐ 10 ☐ 11 ☐ 12 ☐ 13 ☐ 14 ☐ 15 ☐ 16 ☐ 17 ☐ 18 ☐ 19 ☐ 20 ☐ 21 ☐ 22 ☐ 23 ☐ 24 ☐ 25 ☐ 26 ☐ 27 ☐ 28 ☐ 29 ☐ 30 ☐ 31 ☐ 32 ☐ 33 ☐ 34 ☐ 35 ☐ 36 ☐ 37 ☐ 38 ☐ 39 ☐ 40 ☐ 41 ☐ 42 ☐ 43 ☐ 44 ☐ 45 ☐ 46 ☐ 47 ☐ 48 ☐ 49 ☐ 50 ☐

KEY CARDS I HAVE: ____________________

KEY CARDS I NEED: ____________________

COMMENTS: ____________________

OF CARDS I HAVE: ____________

OF CARDS I NEED: ____________

% OF SET FILLED: ____________

50 Card Set

1966 LIONS MARATHON OIL (NFL)

OF CARDS I HAVE:

KEY CARDS I HAVE:

OF CARDS I NEED:

KEY CARDS I NEED:

COMMENTS:

% OF SET FILLED:

7 Card Set

1966 JETS TEAM ISSUE (AFL)

1 2 3 4 5 6 7 8 9

OF CARDS I HAVE:

KEY CARDS I HAVE:

OF CARDS I NEED:

KEY CARDS I NEED:

COMMENTS:

% OF SET FILLED:

9 Card Set

1966 PACKERS MOBIL POSTERS (NFL)

1 2 3 4 5 6 7 8

OF CARDS I HAVE:

KEY CARDS I HAVE:

OF CARDS I NEED:

KEY CARDS I NEED:

COMMENTS:

% OF SET FILLED:

8 Card Set

1966 PHILADELPHIA (NFL)

1	26	51	76	101	126	151	176
2	27	52	77	102	127	152	177
3	28	53	78	103	128	153	178
4	29	54	79	104	129	154	179
5	30	55	80	105	130	155	180
6	31	56	81	106	131	156	181
7	32	57	82	107	132	157	182
8	33	58	83	108	133	158	183
9	34	59	84	109	134	159	184
10	35	60	85	110	135	160	185
11	36	61	86	111	136	161	186
12	37	62	87	112	137	162	187
13	38	63	88	113	138	163	188
14	39	64	89	114	139	164	189
15	40	65	90	115	140	165	190
16	41	66	91	116	141	166	191
17	42	67	92	117	142	167	192
18	43	68	93	118	143	168	193
19	44	69	94	119	144	169	194
20	45	70	95	120	145	170	195
21	46	71	96	121	146	171	196
22	47	72	97	122	147	172	197
23	48	73	98	123	148	173	198
24	49	74	99	124	149	174	
25	50	75	100	125	150	175	

DAVE JONES
LOS ANGELES RAMS END

OF CARDS I HAVE:

OF CARDS I NEED:

% OF SET FILLED:

KEY CARDS I HAVE:

KEY CARDS I NEED:

COMMENTS:

1966 TOPPS FUNNY RINGS (AFL)

1 ☐	11 ☐	21 ☐	☐
2 ☐	12 ☐	22 ☐	☐
3 ☐	13 ☐	23 ☐	☐
4 ☐	14 ☐	24 ☐	☐
5 ☐	15 ☐	☐	☐
6 ☐	16 ☐	☐	☐
7 ☐	17 ☐	☐	☐
8 ☐	18 ☐	☐	☐
9 ☐	19 ☐	☐	☐
10 ☐	20 ☐	☐	☐

KEY CARDS I HAVE: ______________________

OF CARDS I HAVE: ______

OF CARDS I NEED: ______

% OF SET FILLED: ______

KEY CARDS I NEED: ______________________

COMMENTS: ______________________

1966 Topps (AFL)

LEN DAWSON
QUARTERBACK
KANSAS CITY CHIEFS

1 ☐	26 ☐	51 ☐	76 ☐	101 ☐	
2 ☐	27 ☐	52 ☐	77 ☐	102 ☐	
3 ☐	28 ☐	53 ☐	78 ☐	103 ☐	
4 ☐	29 ☐	54 ☐	79 ☐	104 ☐	
5 ☐	30 ☐	55 ☐	80 ☐	105 ☐	
6 ☐	31 ☐	56 ☐	81 ☐	106 ☐	
7 ☐	32 ☐	57 ☐	82 ☐	107 ☐	
8 ☐	33 ☐	58 ☐	83 ☐	108 ☐	
9 ☐	34 ☐	59 ☐	84 ☐	109 ☐	
10 ☐	35 ☐	60 ☐	85 ☐	110 ☐	
11 ☐	36 ☐	61 ☐	86 ☐	111 ☐	
12 ☐	37 ☐	62 ☐	87 ☐	112 ☐	126 ☐
13 ☐	38 ☐	63 ☐	88 ☐	113 ☐	127 ☐
14 ☐	39 ☐	64 ☐	89 ☐	114 ☐	128 ☐
15 ☐	40 ☐	65 ☐	90 ☐	115 ☐	129 ☐
16 ☐	41 ☐	66 ☐	91 ☐	116 ☐	130 ☐
17 ☐	42 ☐	67 ☐	92 ☐	117 ☐	131 ☐
18 ☐	43 ☐	68 ☐	93 ☐	118 ☐	132 ☐
19 ☐	44 ☐	69 ☐	94 ☐	119 ☐	☐
20 ☐	45 ☐	70 ☐	95 ☐	120 ☐	☐
21 ☐	46 ☐	71 ☐	96 ☐	121 ☐	☐
22 ☐	47 ☐	72 ☐	97 ☐	122 ☐	☐
23 ☐	48 ☐	73 ☐	98 ☐	123 ☐	☐
24 ☐	49 ☐	74 ☐	99 ☐	124 ☐	☐
25 ☐	50 ☐	75 ☐	100 ☐	125 ☐	☐

OF CARDS I HAVE: ________

OF CARDS I NEED: ________

% OF SET FILLED: ________

KEY CARDS I HAVE: ________

KEY CARDS I NEED: ________

COMMENTS: ________

1967 COLTS JOHNNY PRO (NFL)

OF CARDS I HAVE:

OF CARDS I NEED:

% OF SET FILLED:

KEY CARDS I HAVE:

KEY CARDS I NEED:

COMMENTS:

1967

1967 BILLS JONES-RICH MILK (AFL)

1 ☐ 2 ☐ 3 ☐ 4 ☐ 5 ☐ 6 ☐ ☐ ☐

OF CARDS I HAVE:

OF CARDS I NEED:

% OF SET FILLED:

KEY CARDS I HAVE:

KEY CARDS I NEED:

COMMENTS:

6 Card Set

1967 DOLPHINS ROYAL CASTLE (AFL)

1 ☐ 2 ☐ 3 ☐ 4 ☐ 5 ☐ 6 ☐ 7 ☐ 8 ☐ 9 ☐ 10 ☐ 11 ☐ 12 ☐ 13 ☐ 14 ☐ 15 ☐ 16 ☐ 17 ☐ 18 ☐ 19 ☐ 20 ☐ 21 ☐ 22 ☐ 23 ☐ 24 ☐ 25 ☐ 26 ☐ 27 ☐ ☐ ☐ ☐

OF CARDS I HAVE:

OF CARDS I NEED:

% OF SET FILLED:

KEY CARDS I HAVE:

KEY CARDS I NEED:

COMMENTS:

27 Card Set

1967 OILERS TEAM ISSUE (AFL)

☐ ☐ ☐ ☐ ☐ ☐ ☐ ☐ ☐ ☐ ☐ ☐ ☐ ☐ ☐ ☐ ☐ ☐ ☐ ☐

OF CARDS I HAVE:

OF CARDS I NEED:

% OF SET FILLED:

KEY CARDS I HAVE:

KEY CARDS I NEED:

COMMENTS:

14 Card Set

1967 PHILADELPHIA (NFL)

1 ☐	26 ☐	51 ☐	76 ☐	101 ☐	126 ☐	151 ☐	176 ☐
2 ☐	27 ☐	52 ☐	77 ☐	102 ☐	127 ☐	152 ☐	177 ☐
3 ☐	28 ☐	53 ☐	78 ☐	103 ☐	128 ☐	153 ☐	178 ☐
4 ☐	29 ☐	54 ☐	79 ☐	104 ☐	129 ☐	154 ☐	179 ☐
5 ☐	30 ☐	55 ☐	80 ☐	105 ☐	130 ☐	155 ☐	180 ☐
6 ☐	31 ☐	56 ☐	81 ☐	106 ☐	131 ☐	156 ☐	181 ☐
7 ☐	32 ☐	57 ☐	82 ☐	107 ☐	132 ☐	157 ☐	182 ☐
8 ☐	33 ☐	58 ☐	83 ☐	108 ☐	133 ☐	158 ☐	183 ☐
9 ☐	34 ☐	59 ☐	84 ☐	109 ☐	134 ☐	159 ☐	184 ☐
10 ☐	35 ☐	60 ☐	85 ☐	110 ☐	135 ☐	160 ☐	185 ☐
11 ☐	36 ☐	61 ☐	86 ☐	111 ☐	136 ☐	161 ☐	186 ☐
12 ☐	37 ☐	62 ☐	87 ☐	112 ☐	137 ☐	162 ☐	187 ☐
13 ☐	38 ☐	63 ☐	88 ☐	113 ☐	138 ☐	163 ☐	188 ☐
14 ☐	39 ☐	64 ☐	89 ☐	114 ☐	139 ☐	164 ☐	189 ☐
15 ☐	40 ☐	65 ☐	90 ☐	115 ☐	140 ☐	165 ☐	190 ☐
16 ☐	41 ☐	66 ☐	91 ☐	116 ☐	141 ☐	166 ☐	191 ☐
17 ☐	42 ☐	67 ☐	92 ☐	117 ☐	142 ☐	167 ☐	192 ☐
18 ☐	43 ☐	68 ☐	93 ☐	118 ☐	143 ☐	168 ☐	193 ☐
19 ☐	44 ☐	69 ☐	94 ☐	119 ☐	144 ☐	169 ☐	194 ☐
20 ☐	45 ☐	70 ☐	95 ☐	120 ☐	145 ☐	170 ☐	195 ☐
21 ☐	46 ☐	71 ☐	96 ☐	121 ☐	146 ☐	171 ☐	196 ☐
22 ☐	47 ☐	72 ☐	97 ☐	122 ☐	147 ☐	172 ☐	197 ☐
23 ☐	48 ☐	73 ☐	98 ☐	123 ☐	148 ☐	173 ☐	198 ☐
24 ☐	49 ☐	74 ☐	99 ☐	124 ☐	149 ☐	174 ☐	☐
25 ☐	50 ☐	75 ☐	100 ☐	125 ☐	150 ☐	175 ☐	☐

GALE SAYERS
CHICAGO BEARS HALFBACK

OF CARDS I HAVE: ____________

OF CARDS I NEED: ____________

% OF SET FILLED: ____________

KEY CARDS I HAVE: ____________

KEY CARDS I NEED: ____________

COMMENTS: ____________

1967 Topps (AFL)

1	☐	26	☐	51	☐	76	☐	101	☐	126	☐
2	☐	27	☐	52	☐	77	☐	102	☐	127	☐
3	☐	28	☐	53	☐	78	☐	103	☐	128	☐
4	☐	29	☐	54	☐	79	☐	104	☐	129	☐
5	☐	30	☐	55	☐	80	☐	105	☐	130	☐
6	☐	31	☐	56	☐	81	☐	106	☐	131	☐
7	☐	32	☐	57	☐	82	☐	107	☐	132	☐
8	☐	33	☐	58	☐	83	☐	108	☐		☐
9	☐	34	☐	59	☐	84	☐	109	☐		☐
10	☐	35	☐	60	☐	85	☐	110	☐		☐
11	☐	36	☐	61	☐	86	☐	111	☐		☐
12	☐	37	☐	62	☐	87	☐	112	☐		☐
13	☐	38	☐	63	☐	88	☐	113	☐		☐
14	☐	39	☐	64	☐	89	☐	114	☐		☐
15	☐	40	☐	65	☐	90	☐	115	☐		☐
16	☐	41	☐	66	☐	91	☐	116	☐		☐
17	☐	42	☐	67	☐	92	☐	117	☐		☐
18	☐	43	☐	68	☐	93	☐	118	☐		☐
19	☐	44	☐	69	☐	94	☐	119	☐		☐
20	☐	45	☐	70	☐	95	☐	120	☐		☐
21	☐	46	☐	71	☐	96	☐	121	☐		☐
22	☐	47	☐	72	☐	97	☐	122	☐		☐
23	☐	48	☐	73	☐	98	☐	123	☐		☐
24	☐	49	☐	74	☐	99	☐	124	☐		☐
25	☐	50	☐	75	☐	100	☐	125	☐		☐

CHIEFS CHIEFS
BOBBY BELL
LINEBACKER

OF CARDS I HAVE: ____________

OF CARDS I NEED: ____________

% OF SET FILLED: ____________

KEY CARDS I HAVE: ____________

KEY CARDS I NEED: ____________

COMMENTS: ____________

1967 WILLIAMS PORTRAITS (NFL)

OF CARDS I HAVE:

OF CARDS I NEED:

% OF SET FILLED:

KEY CARDS I HAVE:

KEY CARDS I NEED:

COMMENTS:

1967 COMIC PENNANTS (NFL)

1	8	15	22	29
2	9	16	23	30
3	10	17	24	31
4	11	18	25	
5	12	19	26	
6	13	20	27	
7	14	21	28	

PEEL OFF PENNANT CAREFULLY 5

MINNEAPOLIS MINI-SKIRTS ARE ON THE RISE

©T.C.G.—PRTD. IN U.S.A.

KEY CARDS I HAVE:

KEY CARDS I NEED:

COMMENTS:

OF CARDS I HAVE:

OF CARDS I NEED:

% OF SET FILLED:

31 Card Set

1967 - 68 VIKINGS (NFL)

1	9	17	25	
2	10	18	26	
3	11	19	27	
4	12	20	28	
5	13	21	29	
6	14	22		
7	15	23		
8	16	24		

KEY CARDS I HAVE:

OF CARDS I HAVE:

KEY CARDS I NEED:

OF CARDS I NEED:

COMMENTS:

% OF SET FILLED:

29 Card Set

1968

1968 FALCONS TEAM ISSUE (NFL)

KEY CARDS I HAVE:

KEY CARDS I NEED:

COMMENTS:

OF CARDS I HAVE:

OF CARDS I NEED:

% OF SET FILLED:

14 Card Set

1968 49ERS WHITE BORDER (NFL)

KEY CARDS I HAVE:

KEY CARDS I NEED:

COMMENTS:

OF CARDS I HAVE:

OF CARDS I NEED:

% OF SET FILLED:

35 Card Set

1968 O-PEE-CHEE (CFL)

1 ☐	26 ☐	51 ☐	76 ☐	101 ☐	126 ☐
2 ☐	27 ☐	52 ☐	77 ☐	102 ☐	127 ☐
3 ☐	28 ☐	53 ☐	78 ☐	103 ☐	128 ☐
4 ☐	29 ☐	54 ☐	79 ☐	104 ☐	129 ☐
5 ☐	30 ☐	55 ☐	80 ☐	105 ☐	130 ☐
6 ☐	31 ☐	56 ☐	81 ☐	106 ☐	131 ☐
7 ☐	32 ☐	57 ☐	82 ☐	107 ☐	132 ☐
8 ☐	33 ☐	58 ☐	83 ☐	108 ☐	☐
9 ☐	34 ☐	59 ☐	84 ☐	109 ☐	☐
10 ☐	35 ☐	60 ☐	85 ☐	110 ☐	☐
11 ☐	36 ☐	61 ☐	86 ☐	111 ☐	☐
12 ☐	37 ☐	62 ☐	87 ☐	112 ☐	☐
13 ☐	38 ☐	63 ☐	88 ☐	113 ☐	☐
14 ☐	39 ☐	64 ☐	89 ☐	114 ☐	☐
15 ☐	40 ☐	65 ☐	90 ☐	115 ☐	☐
16 ☐	41 ☐	66 ☐	91 ☐	116 ☐	☐
17 ☐	42 ☐	67 ☐	92 ☐	117 ☐	☐
18 ☐	43 ☐	68 ☐	93 ☐	118 ☐	☐
19 ☐	44 ☐	69 ☐	94 ☐	119 ☐	☐
20 ☐	45 ☐	70 ☐	95 ☐	120 ☐	☐
21 ☐	46 ☐	71 ☐	96 ☐	121 ☐	☐
22 ☐	47 ☐	72 ☐	97 ☐	122 ☐	☐
23 ☐	48 ☐	73 ☐	98 ☐	123 ☐	☐
24 ☐	49 ☐	74 ☐	99 ☐	124 ☐	☐
25 ☐	50 ☐	75 ☐	100 ☐	125 ☐	☐

WILLIE BETHEA
HAMILTON
TIGER-CATS
BACK

OF CARDS I HAVE: ____________

OF CARDS I NEED: ____________

% OF SET FILLED: ____________

KEY CARDS I HAVE:

KEY CARDS I NEED:

COMMENTS:

1968 O-PEE-CHEE POSTER INSERTS (CFL)

1 ☐ 6 ☐ 11 ☐ 16 ☐
2 ☐ 7 ☐ 12 ☐ ☐
3 ☐ 8 ☐ 13 ☐ ☐
4 ☐ 9 ☐ 14 ☐ ☐
5 ☐ 10 ☐ 15 ☐ ☐

KEY CARDS I HAVE:

KEY CARDS I NEED:

COMMENTS:

16 Card Set

JOE ZUGER
Hamilton Tiger-Cats
QUARTERBACK

OF CARDS I HAVE:

OF CARDS I NEED:

% OF SET FILLED:

1968 STEELERS KDKA (NFL)

1 ☐ 6 ☐ 11 ☐ ☐
2 ☐ 7 ☐ 12 ☐ ☐
3 ☐ 8 ☐ 13 ☐ ☐
4 ☐ 9 ☐ 14 ☐ ☐
5 ☐ 10 ☐ 15 ☐ ☐

KEY CARDS I HAVE:

KEY CARDS I NEED:

COMMENTS:

15 Card Set

CENTERS: John Knight — Ray Mansfield
KDKA

OF CARDS I HAVE:

OF CARDS I NEED:

% OF SET FILLED:

1968 TOPPS INSERTS

1968 TOPPS POSTERS (AFL / NFL)

FRAN TARKENTON
QUARTERBACK
GIANTS

KEY CARDS I HAVE:

KEY CARDS I NEED:

COMMENTS:

OF CARDS I HAVE:

OF CARDS I NEED:

% OF SET FILLED:

16 Card Set

1968 TOPPS STAND-UPS (AFL / NFL)

SONNY JURGENSEN
QUARTERBACK • REDSKINS

KEY CARDS I HAVE:

KEY CARDS I NEED:

COMMENTS:

OF CARDS I HAVE:

OF CARDS I NEED:

% OF SET FILLED:

22 Card Set

1968 Topps (AFL / NFL)

1	26	51	76	101	126	151	176	201
2	27	52	77	102	127	152	177	202
3	28	53	78	103	128	153	178	203
4	29	54	79	104	129	154	179	204
5	30	55	80	105	130	155	180	205
6	31	56	81	106	131	156	181	206
7	32	57	82	107	132	157	182	207
8	33	58	83	108	133	158	183	208
9	34	59	84	109	134	159	184	209
10	35	60	85	110	135	160	185	210
11	36	61	86	111	136	161	186	211
12	37	62	87	112	137	162	187	212
13	38	63	88	113	138	163	188	213
14	39	64	89	114	139	164	189	214
15	40	65	90	115	140	165	190	215
16	41	66	91	116	141	166	191	216
17	42	67	92	117	142	167	192	217
18	43	68	93	118	143	168	193	218
19	44	69	94	119	144	169	194	219
20	45	70	95	120	145	170	195	
21	46	71	96	121	146	171	196	
22	47	72	97	122	147	172	197	
23	48	73	98	123	148	173	198	
24	49	74	99	124	149	174	199	
25	50	75	100	125	150	175	200	

OF CARDS I HAVE: ____________

OF CARDS I NEED: ____________

% OF SET FILLED: ____________

KEY CARDS I HAVE:

KEY CARDS I NEED:

COMMENTS:

1968 TOPPS INSERTS CONT.

1968 TOPPS TEAM PATCH / STICKERS (AFL / NFL)

1 ☐ 11 ☐ 21 ☐ 31 ☐ 41 ☐
2 ☐ 12 ☐ 22 ☐ 32 ☐ 42 ☐
3 ☐ 13 ☐ 23 ☐ 33 ☐ 43 ☐
4 ☐ 14 ☐ 24 ☐ 34 ☐ 44 ☐
5 ☐ 15 ☐ 25 ☐ 35 ☐
6 ☐ 16 ☐ 26 ☐ 36 ☐
7 ☐ 17 ☐ 27 ☐ 37 ☐
8 ☐ 18 ☐ 28 ☐ 38 ☐
9 ☐ 19 ☐ 29 ☐ 39 ☐
10 ☐ 20 ☐ 30 ☐ 40 ☐

KEY CARDS I HAVE: ____________________

KEY CARDS I NEED: ____________________

COMMENTS: ____________________

OF CARDS I HAVE: ____________________

OF CARDS I NEED: ____________________

% OF SET FILLED: ____________________

44 Card Set

1968 TOPPS TEST TEAMS (AFL / NFL)

1 ☐ 6 ☐ 11 ☐ 16 ☐ 21 ☐
2 ☐ 7 ☐ 12 ☐ 17 ☐ 22 ☐
3 ☐ 8 ☐ 13 ☐ 18 ☐ 23 ☐
4 ☐ 9 ☐ 14 ☐ 19 ☐ 24 ☐
5 ☐ 10 ☐ 15 ☐ 20 ☐ 25 ☐

PHILADELPHIA EAGLES

KEY CARDS I HAVE: ____________________

KEY CARDS I NEED: ____________________

COMMENTS: ____________________

OF CARDS I HAVE: ____________________

OF CARDS I NEED: ____________________

% OF SET FILLED: ____________________

25 Card Set

1968 - 69 SAINTS 8 X 10 (NFL)

OF CARDS I HAVE:

KEY CARDS I HAVE:

OF CARDS I NEED:

KEY CARDS I NEED:

COMMENTS:

% OF SET FILLED:

35 Card Set

1969 MARYLAND TEAM SHEETS (COLLEGE)

OF CARDS I HAVE:

1 3 5
2 4 6

KEY CARDS I HAVE:

OF CARDS I NEED:

KEY CARDS I NEED:

COMMENTS:

% OF SET FILLED:

6 Card Set

1969 SOUTH CAROLINA TEAM SHEETS (COLLEGE)

1 3 5
2 4 6

OF CARDS I HAVE:

KEY CARDS I HAVE:

OF CARDS I NEED:

KEY CARDS I NEED:

COMMENTS:

% OF SET FILLED:

6 Card Set

1968 - 70

1968 AMERICAN OIL MR. & MRS. (NFL)

1 ☐ 4 ☐ 7 ☐ 10 ☐ 13 ☐ 16 ☐
2 ☐ 5 ☐ 8 ☐ 11 ☐ 14 ☐ ☐
3 ☐ 6 ☐ 9 ☐ 12 ☐ 15 ☐ ☐

OF CARDS I HAVE: ____________

KEY CARDS I HAVE: ____________

OF CARDS I NEED: ____________

KEY CARDS I NEED: ____________

COMMENTS: ____________

% OF SET FILLED: ____________

16 Card Set

1968 BENGALS TEAM ISSUE (AFL)

1 ☐ 3 ☐ 5 ☐ 7 ☐ ☐
2 ☐ 4 ☐ 6 ☐ ☐ ☐

OF CARDS I HAVE: ____________

KEY CARDS I HAVE: ____________

OF CARDS I NEED: ____________

KEY CARDS I NEED: ____________

COMMENTS: ____________

% OF SET FILLED: ____________

7 Card Set

1968 - 70 BRONCOS (AFL)

OF CARDS I HAVE: ____________

OF CARDS I NEED: ____________

KEY CARDS I HAVE: ____________

KEY CARDS I NEED: ____________

% OF SET FILLED: ____________

COMMENTS: ____________

53 Card Set

1969

1969 BENGALS TRESLER COMET (AFL)

KEY CARDS I HAVE:

KEY CARDS I NEED:

COMMENTS:

OF CARDS I HAVE:

OF CARDS I NEED:

% OF SET FILLED:

20 Card Set

1969 CHIEFS KROGER (AFL)

1
2
3
4
5
6
7
8

WILLIE LANIER

KEY CARDS I HAVE:

KEY CARDS I NEED:

COMMENTS:

OF CARDS I HAVE:

OF CARDS I NEED:

% OF SET FILLED:

8 Card Set

1969 COWBOYS TEAM ISSUE (NFL)

OF CARDS I HAVE:

KEY CARDS I HAVE:

OF CARDS I NEED:

KEY CARDS I NEED:

COMMENTS:

% OF SET FILLED:

5 Card Set

1969 ESKIMO PIE (AFL)

OF CARDS I HAVE:

OF CARDS I NEED:

KEY CARDS I HAVE:

KEY CARDS I NEED:

COMMENTS:

% OF SET FILLED:

15 Card Set

1969 JETS TASCO PRINTS (AFL)

OF CARDS I HAVE:

1 3 5
2 4 6

KEY CARDS I HAVE:

OF CARDS I NEED:

KEY CARDS I NEED:

COMMENTS:

% OF SET FILLED:

6 Card Set

1969 OILERS TEAM ISSUE (AFL)

OF CARDS I HAVE:

KEY CARDS I HAVE:

OF CARDS I NEED:

KEY CARDS I NEED:

COMMENTS:

% OF SET FILLED:

39 Card Set

1969 GLENDALE STAMPS (AFL / NFL)

OF CARDS I HAVE:

OF CARDS I NEED:

% OF SET FILLED:

KEY CARDS I HAVE:

KEY CARDS I NEED:

COMMENTS:

1969 CONT. 2

1969 PACKERS DRENKS POTATO CHIP PINS (NFL)

1 ☐	6 ☐	11 ☐	16 ☐	☐
2 ☐	7 ☐	12 ☐	17 ☐	☐
3 ☐	8 ☐	13 ☐	18 ☐	☐
4 ☐	9 ☐	14 ☐	19 ☐	☐
5 ☐	10 ☐	15 ☐	20 ☐	☐

KEY CARDS I HAVE: ______

KEY CARDS I NEED: ______

COMMENTS: ______

______

OF CARDS I HAVE: ______

OF CARDS I NEED: ______

% OF SET FILLED: ______

20 Card Set

1969 PACKERS TASCO PRINTS (NFL)

1 ☐	3 ☐	5 ☐	7 ☐	☐
2 ☐	4 ☐	6 ☐	☐	☐

KEY CARDS I HAVE: ______

KEY CARDS I NEED: ______

COMMENTS: ______

______

OF CARDS I HAVE: ______

OF CARDS I NEED: ______

% OF SET FILLED: ______

7 Card Set

1969 REDSKINS HIGH'S DAIRY (NFL)

☐	☐	☐	☐	☐
☐	☐	☐	☐	☐

KEY CARDS I HAVE: ______

KEY CARDS I NEED: ______

COMMENTS: ______

______

OF CARDS I HAVE: ______

OF CARDS I NEED: ______

% OF SET FILLED: ______

8 Card Set

1969 TOPPS FOUR IN ONES (AFL / NFL)

OF CARDS I HAVE:

OF CARDS I NEED:

% OF SET FILLED:

KEY CARDS I HAVE:

KEY CARDS I NEED:

COMMENTS:

1969 TOPPS (AFL / NFL)

1 ☐	26 ☐	51 ☐	76 ☐	101 ☐	126 ☐	151 ☐	176 ☐	201 ☐	226 ☐	251 ☐
2 ☐	27 ☐	52 ☐	77 ☐	102 ☐	127 ☐	152 ☐	177 ☐	202 ☐	227 ☐	252 ☐
3 ☐	28 ☐	53 ☐	78 ☐	103 ☐	128 ☐	153 ☐	178 ☐	203 ☐	228 ☐	253 ☐
4 ☐	29 ☐	54 ☐	79 ☐	104 ☐	129 ☐	154 ☐	179 ☐	204 ☐	229 ☐	254 ☐
5 ☐	30 ☐	55 ☐	80 ☐	105 ☐	130 ☐	155 ☐	180 ☐	205 ☐	230 ☐	255 ☐
6 ☐	31 ☐	56 ☐	81 ☐	106 ☐	131 ☐	156 ☐	181 ☐	206 ☐	231 ☐	256 ☐
7 ☐	32 ☐	57 ☐	82 ☐	107 ☐	132 ☐	157 ☐	182 ☐	207 ☐	232 ☐	257 ☐
8 ☐	33 ☐	58 ☐	83 ☐	108 ☐	133 ☐	158 ☐	183 ☐	208 ☐	233 ☐	258 ☐
9 ☐	34 ☐	59 ☐	84 ☐	109 ☐	134 ☐	159 ☐	184 ☐	209 ☐	234 ☐	259 ☐
10 ☐	35 ☐	60 ☐	85 ☐	110 ☐	135 ☐	160 ☐	185 ☐	210 ☐	235 ☐	260 ☐
11 ☐	36 ☐	61 ☐	86 ☐	111 ☐	136 ☐	161 ☐	186 ☐	211 ☐	236 ☐	261 ☐
12 ☐	37 ☐	62 ☐	87 ☐	112 ☐	137 ☐	162 ☐	187 ☐	212 ☐	237 ☐	262 ☐
13 ☐	38 ☐	63 ☐	88 ☐	113 ☐	138 ☐	163 ☐	188 ☐	213 ☐	238 ☐	263 ☐
14 ☐	39 ☐	64 ☐	89 ☐	114 ☐	139 ☐	164 ☐	189 ☐	214 ☐	239 ☐	☐
15 ☐	40 ☐	65 ☐	90 ☐	115 ☐	140 ☐	165 ☐	190 ☐	215 ☐	240 ☐	☐
16 ☐	41 ☐	66 ☐	91 ☐	116 ☐	141 ☐	166 ☐	191 ☐	216 ☐	241 ☐	☐
17 ☐	42 ☐	67 ☐	92 ☐	117 ☐	142 ☐	167 ☐	192 ☐	217 ☐	242 ☐	☐
18 ☐	43 ☐	68 ☐	93 ☐	118 ☐	143 ☐	168 ☐	193 ☐	218 ☐	243 ☐	☐
19 ☐	44 ☐	69 ☐	94 ☐	119 ☐	144 ☐	169 ☐	194 ☐	219 ☐	244 ☐	☐
20 ☐	45 ☐	70 ☐	95 ☐	120 ☐	145 ☐	170 ☐	195 ☐	220 ☐	245 ☐	☐
21 ☐	46 ☐	71 ☐	96 ☐	121 ☐	146 ☐	171 ☐	196 ☐	221 ☐	246 ☐	☐
22 ☐	47 ☐	72 ☐	97 ☐	122 ☐	147 ☐	172 ☐	197 ☐	222 ☐	247 ☐	☐
23 ☐	48 ☐	73 ☐	98 ☐	123 ☐	148 ☐	173 ☐	198 ☐	223 ☐	248 ☐	☐
24 ☐	49 ☐	74 ☐	99 ☐	124 ☐	149 ☐	174 ☐	199 ☐	224 ☐	249 ☐	☐
25 ☐	50 ☐	75 ☐	100 ☐	125 ☐	150 ☐	175 ☐	200 ☐	225 ☐	250 ☐	☐

Bryon
PICCOLO
CHICAGO BEARS • RUNNING BACK

OF CARDS I HAVE: ____________

OF CARDS I NEED: ____________

% OF SET FILLED: ____________

KEY CARDS I HAVE: ____________

KEY CARDS I NEED: ____________

COMMENTS: ____________

1969 TOPPS MINI-ALBUMS (AFL / NFL)

1	6	11	16	21	26
2	7	12	17	22	
3	8	13	18	23	
4	9	14	19	24	
5	10	15	20	25	

KEY CARDS I HAVE:

KEY CARDS I NEED:

COMMENTS:

OF CARDS I HAVE:

OF CARDS I NEED:

% OF SET FILLED:

26 Card Set

1969 VIKINGS TEAM ISSUE (NFL)

1	6	11	16	21	26
2	7	12	17	22	27
3	8	13	18	23	
4	9	14	19	24	
5	10	15	20	25	

KEY CARDS I HAVE:

KEY CARDS I NEED:

COMMENTS:

OF CARDS I HAVE:

OF CARDS I NEED:

% OF SET FILLED:

27 Card Set

1970 CLARK VOLPE (NFL)

1 ☐ 2 ☐ 3 ☐ 4 ☐ 5 ☐ 6 ☐ 7 ☐ 8 ☐ 9 ☐ 10 ☐ 11 ☐ 12 ☐
13 ☐ 14 ☐ 15 ☐ 16 ☐ 17 ☐ 18 ☐ 19 ☐ 20 ☐ 21 ☐ 22 ☐ 23 ☐ 24 ☐
25 ☐ 26 ☐ 27 ☐ 28 ☐ 29 ☐ 30 ☐ 31 ☐ 32 ☐ 33 ☐ 34 ☐ 35 ☐ 36 ☐
37 ☐ 38 ☐ 39 ☐ 40 ☐ 41 ☐ 42 ☐ 43 ☐ 44 ☐ 45 ☐ 46 ☐ 47 ☐ 48 ☐
49 ☐ 50 ☐ 51 ☐ 52 ☐ 53 ☐ 54 ☐ 55 ☐ 56 ☐ 57 ☐ 58 ☐ 59 ☐ 60 ☐
61 ☐ 62 ☐ 63 ☐ 64 ☐ 65 ☐ 66 ☐

KEY CARDS I HAVE:

OF CARDS I HAVE:

KEY CARDS I NEED:

OF CARDS I NEED:

COMMENTS:

% OF SET FILLED:

66 Card Set

1970 HI-C POSTERS (NFL)

1 ☐ 2 ☐ 3 ☐
4 ☐ 5 ☐ 6 ☐
7 ☐ 8 ☐ 9 ☐
10 ☐

KEY CARDS I HAVE:

OF CARDS I HAVE:

KEY CARDS I NEED:

OF CARDS I NEED:

COMMENTS:

% OF SET FILLED:

10 Card Set

1970 KELLOGG'S (NFL)

1	☐	16	☐	31	☐	46	☐
2	☐	17	☐	32	☐	47	☐
3	☐	18	☐	33	☐	48	☐
4	☐	19	☐	34	☐	49	☐
5	☐	20	☐	35	☐	50	☐
6	☐	21	☐	36	☐	51	☐
7	☐	22	☐	37	☐	52	☐
8	☐	23	☐	38	☐	53	☐
9	☐	24	☐	39	☐	54	☐
10	☐	25	☐	40	☐	55	☐
11	☐	26	☐	41	☐	56	☐
12	☐	27	☐	42	☐	57	☐
13	☐	28	☐	43	☐	58	☐
14	☐	29	☐	44	☐	59	☐
15	☐	30	☐	45	☐	60	☐

BUBBA SMITH

OF CARDS I HAVE: ____________

OF CARDS I NEED: ____________

% OF SET FILLED: ____________

KEY CARDS I HAVE: ____________

KEY CARDS I NEED: ____________

COMMENTS: ____________

1970 O-PEE-CHEE (CFL)

1 ☐	26 ☐	51 ☐	76 ☐	101 ☐
2 ☐	27 ☐	52 ☐	77 ☐	102 ☐
3 ☐	28 ☐	53 ☐	78 ☐	103 ☐
4 ☐	29 ☐	54 ☐	79 ☐	104 ☐
5 ☐	30 ☐	55 ☐	80 ☐	105 ☐
6 ☐	31 ☐	56 ☐	81 ☐	106 ☐
7 ☐	32 ☐	57 ☐	82 ☐	107 ☐
8 ☐	33 ☐	58 ☐	83 ☐	108 ☐
9 ☐	34 ☐	59 ☐	84 ☐	109 ☐
10 ☐	35 ☐	60 ☐	85 ☐	110 ☐
11 ☐	36 ☐	61 ☐	86 ☐	111 ☐
12 ☐	37 ☐	62 ☐	87 ☐	112 ☐
13 ☐	38 ☐	63 ☐	88 ☐	113 ☐
14 ☐	39 ☐	64 ☐	89 ☐	114 ☐
15 ☐	40 ☐	65 ☐	90 ☐	115 ☐
16 ☐	41 ☐	66 ☐	91 ☐	☐
17 ☐	42 ☐	67 ☐	92 ☐	☐
18 ☐	43 ☐	68 ☐	93 ☐	☐
19 ☐	44 ☐	69 ☐	94 ☐	☐
20 ☐	45 ☐	70 ☐	95 ☐	☐
21 ☐	46 ☐	71 ☐	96 ☐	☐
22 ☐	47 ☐	72 ☐	97 ☐	☐
23 ☐	48 ☐	73 ☐	98 ☐	☐
24 ☐	49 ☐	74 ☐	99 ☐	☐
25 ☐	50 ☐	75 ☐	100 ☐	☐

Moses
DENSON
Montreal Alouettes • Running Back

OF CARDS I HAVE: ____________

OF CARDS I NEED: ____________

% OF SET FILLED: ____________

KEY CARDS I HAVE: ____________

KEY CARDS I NEED: ____________

COMMENTS: ____________

1970 TOPPS POSTERS (NFL)

1 ☐	6 ☐	11 ☐	16 ☐	21 ☐
2 ☐	7 ☐	12 ☐	17 ☐	22 ☐
3 ☐	8 ☐	13 ☐	18 ☐	23 ☐
4 ☐	9 ☐	14 ☐	19 ☐	24 ☐
5 ☐	10 ☐	15 ☐	20 ☐	☐

KEY CARDS I HAVE: ______

KEY CARDS I NEED: ______

COMMENTS: ______

OF CARDS I HAVE: ______

OF CARDS I NEED: ______

% OF SET FILLED: ______

24 Card Set

1970 O-PEE-CHEE PUSH OUT INSERTS (CFL)

1 ☐	5 ☐	9 ☐	13 ☐	☐
2 ☐	6 ☐	10 ☐	14 ☐	☐
3 ☐	7 ☐	11 ☐	15 ☐	☐
4 ☐	8 ☐	12 ☐	16 ☐	☐

KEY CARDS I HAVE: ______

KEY CARDS I NEED: ______

COMMENTS: ______

OF CARDS I HAVE: ______

OF CARDS I NEED: ______

% OF SET FILLED: ______

16 Card Set

1970 Topps (NFL)

1	26	51	76	101	126	151	176	201	226	251
2	27	52	77	102	127	152	177	202	227	252
3	28	53	78	103	128	153	178	203	228	253
4	29	54	79	104	129	154	179	204	229	254
5	30	55	80	105	130	155	180	205	230	255
6	31	56	81	106	131	156	181	206	231	256
7	32	57	82	107	132	157	182	207	232	257
8	33	58	83	108	133	158	183	208	233	258
9	34	59	84	109	134	159	184	209	234	259
10	35	60	85	110	135	160	185	210	235	260
11	36	61	86	111	136	161	186	211	236	261
12	37	62	87	112	137	162	187	212	237	262
13	38	63	88	113	138	163	188	213	238	263
14	39	64	89	114	139	164	189	214	239	
15	40	65	90	115	140	165	190	215	240	
16	41	66	91	116	141	166	191	216	241	
17	42	67	92	117	142	167	192	217	242	
18	43	68	93	118	143	168	193	218	243	
19	44	69	94	119	144	169	194	219	244	
20	45	70	95	120	145	170	195	220	245	
21	46	71	96	121	146	171	196	221	246	
22	47	72	97	122	147	172	197	222	247	
23	48	73	98	123	148	173	198	223	248	
24	49	74	99	124	149	174	199	224	249	
25	50	75	100	125	150	175	200	225	250	

BUCK BUCHANAN
CHIEFS
DEFENSIVE TACKLE

OF CARDS I HAVE:

OF CARDS I NEED:

% OF SET FILLED:

KEY CARDS I HAVE:

KEY CARDS I NEED:

COMMENTS:

1970 TOPPS SUPER INSERTS

1970 TOPPS SUPER GLOSSY (NFL)

FLOYD LITTLE
running back Broncos

1 ☐	8 ☐	15 ☐	22 ☐	29 ☐
2 ☐	9 ☐	16 ☐	23 ☐	30 ☐
3 ☐	10 ☐	17 ☐	24 ☐	31 ☐
4 ☐	11 ☐	18 ☐	25 ☐	32 ☐
5 ☐	12 ☐	19 ☐	26 ☐	33 ☐
6 ☐	13 ☐	20 ☐	27 ☐	☐
7 ☐	14 ☐	21 ☐	28 ☐	☐

KEY CARDS I HAVE: ____________________

KEY CARDS I NEED: ____________________

COMMENTS: ____________________

OF CARDS I HAVE: __________

OF CARDS I NEED: __________

% OF SET FILLED: __________

33 Card Set

1970 TOPPS SUPERS (NFL)

John Brodie

1 ☐	9 ☐	17 ☐	25 ☐	33 ☐
2 ☐	10 ☐	18 ☐	26 ☐	34 ☐
3 ☐	11 ☐	19 ☐	27 ☐	35 ☐
4 ☐	12 ☐	20 ☐	28 ☐	☐
5 ☐	13 ☐	21 ☐	29 ☐	☐
6 ☐	14 ☐	22 ☐	30 ☐	☐
7 ☐	15 ☐	23 ☐	31 ☐	☐
8 ☐	16 ☐	24 ☐	32 ☐	☐

KEY CARDS I HAVE: ____________________

KEY CARDS I NEED: ____________________

COMMENTS: ____________________

OF CARDS I HAVE: __________

OF CARDS I NEED: __________

% OF SET FILLED: __________

35 Card Set

1971 ALABAMA TEAM SHEETS (COLLEGE)

1 ☐ 3 ☐ 5 ☐ ☐
2 ☐ 4 ☐ 6 ☐ ☐

KEY CARDS I HAVE: ________ # OF CARDS I HAVE: ________

KEY CARDS I NEED: ________ # OF CARDS I NEED: ________

COMMENTS: ________ % OF SET FILLED: ________

6 Card Set

1971 COWBOYS TEAM ISSUE (NFL)

KEY CARDS I HAVE: ________ # OF CARDS I HAVE: ________

KEY CARDS I NEED: ________ # OF CARDS I NEED: ________

COMMENTS: ________ % OF SET FILLED: ________

40 Card Set

1971 BAZOOKA (NFL)

1 ☐	9 ☐	17 ☐	25 ☐	33 ☐
2 ☐	10 ☐	18 ☐	26 ☐	34 ☐
3 ☐	11 ☐	19 ☐	27 ☐	35 ☐
4 ☐	12 ☐	20 ☐	28 ☐	36 ☐
5 ☐	13 ☐	21 ☐	29 ☐	☐
6 ☐	14 ☐	22 ☐	30 ☐	☐
7 ☐	15 ☐	23 ☐	31 ☐	☐
8 ☐	16 ☐	24 ☐	32 ☐	☐

KEY CARDS I HAVE: ____________________

KEY CARDS I NEED: ____________________

COMMENTS: ____________________

OF CARDS I HAVE: __________

OF CARDS I NEED: __________

% OF SET FILLED: __________

36 Card Set

1971 CHIEFS TEAM ISSUE (NFL)

1 ☐	4 ☐	7 ☐	10 ☐	☐
2 ☐	5 ☐	8 ☐	☐	☐
3 ☐	6 ☐	9 ☐	☐	☐

KEY CARDS I HAVE: ____________________

KEY CARDS I NEED: ____________________

COMMENTS: ____________________

OF CARDS I HAVE: __________

OF CARDS I NEED: __________

% OF SET FILLED: __________

10 Card Set

1971 CFL

1971 CHEVRON B.C. LIONS (CFL)

1 ☐	13 ☐	25 ☐	37 ☐	49 ☐
2 ☐	14 ☐	26 ☐	38 ☐	50 ☐
3 ☐	15 ☐	27 ☐	39 ☐	☐
4 ☐	16 ☐	28 ☐	40 ☐	☐
5 ☐	17 ☐	29 ☐	41 ☐	☐
6 ☐	18 ☐	30 ☐	42 ☐	☐
7 ☐	19 ☐	31 ☐	43 ☐	☐
8 ☐	20 ☐	32 ☐	44 ☐	☐
9 ☐	21 ☐	33 ☐	45 ☐	☐
10 ☐	22 ☐	34 ☐	46 ☐	☐
11 ☐	23 ☐	35 ☐	47 ☐	☐
12 ☐	24 ☐	36 ☐	48 ☐	☐

KEY CARDS I HAVE: ______________________________

____

KEY CARDS I NEED: ______________________________

____

COMMENTS: ______________________________

____

OF CARDS I HAVE: __________

OF CARDS I NEED: __________

% OF SET FILLED: __________

50 Card set

1971 CHIQUITA CFL ALL-STARS (CFL)

1 ☐	7 ☐	13 ☐	19 ☐	25 ☐
3 ☐	9 ☐	15 ☐	21 ☐	☐
5 ☐	11 ☐	17 ☐	23 ☐	☐

KEY CARDS I HAVE: ______________________________

____

KEY CARDS I NEED: ______________________________

____

COMMENTS: ______________________________

____

OF CARDS I HAVE: __________

OF CARDS I NEED: __________

% OF SET FILLED: __________

13 Card set

1971 KELLOGG'S (NFL)

1 ☐	16 ☐	31 ☐	46 ☐	☐
2 ☐	17 ☐	32 ☐	47 ☐	☐
3 ☐	18 ☐	33 ☐	48 ☐	☐
4 ☐	19 ☐	34 ☐	49 ☐	☐
5 ☐	20 ☐	35 ☐	50 ☐	☐
6 ☐	21 ☐	36 ☐	51 ☐	☐
7 ☐	22 ☐	37 ☐	52 ☐	☐
8 ☐	23 ☐	38 ☐	53 ☐	☐
9 ☐	24 ☐	39 ☐	54 ☐	☐
10 ☐	25 ☐	40 ☐	55 ☐	☐
11 ☐	26 ☐	41 ☐	56 ☐	☐
12 ☐	27 ☐	42 ☐	57 ☐	☐
13 ☐	28 ☐	43 ☐	58 ☐	☐
14 ☐	29 ☐	44 ☐	59 ☐	☐
15 ☐	30 ☐	45 ☐	60 ☐	☐

\# OF CARDS I HAVE: ____________

\# OF CARDS I NEED: ____________

% OF SET FILLED: ____________

KEY CARDS I HAVE: ____________

KEY CARDS I NEED: ____________

COMMENTS: ____________

1971 EAGLES TEAM ISSUE (NFL)

KEY CARDS I HAVE:

KEY CARDS I NEED:

COMMENTS:

OF CARDS I HAVE:

OF CARDS I NEED:

% OF SET FILLED:

16 Card Set

1971 IOWA TEAM PHOTOS (COLLEGE)

1
2
3
4

KEY CARDS I HAVE:

KEY CARDS I NEED:

COMMENTS:

OF CARDS I HAVE:

OF CARDS I NEED:

% OF SET FILLED:

4 Card Set

1971 MATTEL MINI-RECORDS (NFL)

1 5 9 13 17
2 6 10 14
3 7 11 15
4 8 12 16

DICK
BUTKUS
Chicago Bears

KEY CARDS I HAVE:

KEY CARDS I NEED:

COMMENTS:

OF CARDS I HAVE:

OF CARDS I NEED:

% OF SET FILLED:

17 Card Set

1971 O-PEE-CHEE (CFL)

1 ☐	26 ☐	51 ☐	76 ☐	101 ☐	126 ☐
2 ☐	27 ☐	52 ☐	77 ☐	102 ☐	127 ☐
3 ☐	28 ☐	53 ☐	78 ☐	103 ☐	128 ☐
4 ☐	29 ☐	54 ☐	79 ☐	104 ☐	129 ☐
5 ☐	30 ☐	55 ☐	80 ☐	105 ☐	130 ☐
6 ☐	31 ☐	56 ☐	81 ☐	106 ☐	131 ☐
7 ☐	32 ☐	57 ☐	82 ☐	107 ☐	132 ☐
8 ☐	33 ☐	58 ☐	83 ☐	108 ☐	☐
9 ☐	34 ☐	59 ☐	84 ☐	109 ☐	☐
10 ☐	35 ☐	60 ☐	85 ☐	110 ☐	☐
11 ☐	36 ☐	61 ☐	86 ☐	111 ☐	☐
12 ☐	37 ☐	62 ☐	87 ☐	112 ☐	☐
13 ☐	38 ☐	63 ☐	88 ☐	113 ☐	☐
14 ☐	39 ☐	64 ☐	89 ☐	114 ☐	☐
15 ☐	40 ☐	65 ☐	90 ☐	115 ☐	☐
16 ☐	41 ☐	66 ☐	91 ☐	116 ☐	☐
17 ☐	42 ☐	67 ☐	92 ☐	117 ☐	☐
18 ☐	43 ☐	68 ☐	93 ☐	118 ☐	☐
19 ☐	44 ☐	69 ☐	94 ☐	119 ☐	☐
20 ☐	45 ☐	70 ☐	95 ☐	120 ☐	☐
21 ☐	46 ☐	71 ☐	96 ☐	121 ☐	☐
22 ☐	47 ☐	72 ☐	97 ☐	122 ☐	☐
23 ☐	48 ☐	73 ☐	98 ☐	123 ☐	☐
24 ☐	49 ☐	74 ☐	99 ☐	124 ☐	☐
25 ☐	50 ☐	75 ☐	100 ☐	125 ☐	☐

JOE THEISMANN
TORONTO
Argonauts
QUARTERBACK

OF CARDS I HAVE: ______________

OF CARDS I NEED: ______________

% OF SET FILLED: ______________

KEY CARDS I HAVE: ____

KEY CARDS I NEED: ____

COMMENTS: ____

1971 O-PEE-CHEE CFL POSTER INSERTS (CFL)

1 ☐ 6 ☐ 11 ☐ 16 ☐
2 ☐ 7 ☐ 12 ☐
3 ☐ 8 ☐ 13 ☐
4 ☐ 9 ☐ 14 ☐
5 ☐ 10 ☐ 15 ☐

KEY CARDS I HAVE:

\# OF CARDS I HAVE:

KEY CARDS I NEED:

\# OF CARDS I NEED:

COMMENTS:

% OF SET FILLED:

16 Card Set

1971 OILERS TEAM ISSUE (NFL)

KEY CARDS I HAVE:

\# OF CARDS I HAVE:

KEY CARDS I NEED:

\# OF CARDS I NEED:

COMMENTS:

% OF SET FILLED:

23 Card Set

1971 Topps (NFL)

1	26	51	76	101	126	151	176	201	226	251
2	27	52	77	102	127	152	177	202	227	252
3	28	53	78	103	128	153	178	203	228	253
4	29	54	79	104	129	154	179	204	229	254
5	30	55	80	105	130	155	180	205	230	255
6	31	56	81	106	131	156	181	206	231	256
7	32	57	82	107	132	157	182	207	232	257
8	33	58	83	108	133	158	183	208	233	258
9	34	59	84	109	134	159	184	209	234	259
10	35	60	85	110	135	160	185	210	235	260
11	36	61	86	111	136	161	186	211	236	261
12	37	62	87	112	137	162	187	212	237	262
13	38	63	88	113	138	163	188	213	238	263
14	39	64	89	114	139	164	189	214	239	
15	40	65	90	115	140	165	190	215	240	
16	41	66	91	116	141	166	191	216	241	
17	42	67	92	117	142	167	192	217	242	
18	43	68	93	118	143	168	193	218	243	
19	44	69	94	119	144	169	194	219	244	
20	45	70	95	120	145	170	195	220	245	
21	46	71	96	121	146	171	196	221	246	
22	47	72	97	122	147	172	197	222	247	
23	48	73	98	123	148	173	198	223	248	
24	49	74	99	124	149	174	199	224	249	
25	50	75	100	125	150	175	200	225	250	

OF CARDS I HAVE: ______

OF CARDS I NEED: ______

% OF SET FILLED: ______

KEY CARDS I HAVE: ______

KEY CARDS I NEED: ______

COMMENTS: ______

1971 TOPPS INSERTS

1971 TOPPS GAME CARDS (NFL)

1 ☐	11 ☐	21 ☐	31 ☐	41 ☐	51 ☐
2 ☐	12 ☐	22 ☐	32 ☐	42 ☐	52 ☐
3 ☐	13 ☐	23 ☐	33 ☐	43 ☐	53 ☐
4 ☐	14 ☐	24 ☐	34 ☐	44 ☐	☐
5 ☐	15 ☐	25 ☐	35 ☐	45 ☐	☐
6 ☐	16 ☐	26 ☐	36 ☐	46 ☐	☐
7 ☐	17 ☐	27 ☐	37 ☐	47 ☐	☐
8 ☐	18 ☐	28 ☐	38 ☐	48 ☐	☐
9 ☐	19 ☐	29 ☐	39 ☐	49 ☐	☐
10 ☐	20 ☐	30 ☐	40 ☐	50 ☐	☐

KEY CARDS I HAVE: ____________________

KEY CARDS I NEED: ____________________

COMMENTS: ____________________

OF CARDS I HAVE: __________

OF CARDS I NEED: __________

% OF SET FILLED: __________

53 Card Set

1971 TOPPS POSTERS (NFL)

1 ☐	7 ☐	13 ☐	19 ☐	25 ☐	31 ☐
2 ☐	8 ☐	14 ☐	20 ☐	26 ☐	32 ☐
3 ☐	9 ☐	15 ☐	21 ☐	27 ☐	☐
4 ☐	10 ☐	16 ☐	22 ☐	28 ☐	☐
5 ☐	11 ☐	17 ☐	23 ☐	29 ☐	☐
6 ☐	12 ☐	18 ☐	24 ☐	30 ☐	☐

KEY CARDS I HAVE: ____________________

KEY CARDS I NEED: ____________________

COMMENTS: ____________________

OF CARDS I HAVE: __________

OF CARDS I NEED: __________

% OF SET FILLED: __________

32 Card Set

1971 VIKINGS

1971 VIKINGS PHOTOS (NFL)

1 ☐	11 ☐	21 ☐	31 ☐	41 ☐	51 ☐
2 ☐	12 ☐	22 ☐	32 ☐	42 ☐	52 ☐
3 ☐	13 ☐	23 ☐	33 ☐	43 ☐	☐
4 ☐	14 ☐	24 ☐	34 ☐	44 ☐	☐
5 ☐	15 ☐	25 ☐	35 ☐	45 ☐	☐
6 ☐	16 ☐	26 ☐	36 ☐	46 ☐	☐
7 ☐	17 ☐	27 ☐	37 ☐	47 ☐	☐
8 ☐	18 ☐	28 ☐	38 ☐	48 ☐	☐
9 ☐	19 ☐	29 ☐	39 ☐	49 ☐	☐
10 ☐	20 ☐	30 ☐	40 ☐	50 ☐	☐

KEY CARDS I HAVE: ________________ # OF CARDS I HAVE: ________

KEY CARDS I NEED: ________________ # OF CARDS I NEED: ________

COMMENTS: ________________ % OF SET FILLED: ________

52 Card Set

1971 VIKINGS POSTCARDS (NFL)

1 ☐	6 ☐	11 ☐	16 ☐	☐
2 ☐	7 ☐	12 ☐	17 ☐	☐
3 ☐	8 ☐	13 ☐	18 ☐	☐
4 ☐	9 ☐	14 ☐	19 ☐	☐
5 ☐	10 ☐	15 ☐	☐	☐

KEY CARDS I HAVE: ________________ # OF CARDS I HAVE: ________

KEY CARDS I NEED: ________________ # OF CARDS I NEED: ________

COMMENTS: ________________ % OF SET FILLED: ________

19 Card Set

1971 - 72 DELL (NFL)

BOB HAYES
Dallas

KEY CARDS I HAVE:

OF CARDS I HAVE:

KEY CARDS I NEED:

OF CARDS I NEED:

COMMENTS:

% OF SET FILLED:

48 Card Set

1972 BAZOOKA OFFICIAL SIGNALS (NFL)

1 2 3 4 5 6 7 8 9 10 11 12

KEY CARDS I HAVE:

OF CARDS I HAVE:

KEY CARDS I NEED:

OF CARDS I NEED:

COMMENTS:

% OF SET FILLED:

12 Card Set

1972

1972 ALABAMA (COLLEGE)

1C ☐	4C ☐	7C ☐	10C ☐	13C ☐
1D ☐	4D ☐	7D ☐	10D ☐	13D ☐
1H ☐	4H ☐	7H ☐	10H ☐	13H ☐
1S ☐	4S ☐	7S ☐	10S ☐	13S ☐
2C ☐	5C ☐	8C ☐	11C ☐	JK ☐
2D ☐	5D ☐	8D ☐	11D ☐	JK ☐
2H ☐	5H ☐	8H ☐	11H ☐	☐
2S ☐	5S ☐	8S ☐	11S ☐	☐
3C ☐	6C ☐	9C ☐	12C ☐	☐
3D ☐	6D ☐	9D ☐	12D ☐	☐
3H ☐	6H ☐	9H ☐	12H ☐	☐
3S ☐	6S ☐	9S ☐	12S ☐	☐

KEY CARDS I HAVE: ______________________

OF CARDS I HAVE: ______________________

KEY CARDS I NEED: ______________________

OF CARDS I NEED: ______________________

COMMENTS: ______________________

% OF SET FILLED: ______________________

54 Card Set

1972 CHIQUITA NFL SLIDES (NFL)

1 ☐	7 ☐	13 ☐	19 ☐	25 ☐
3 ☐	9 ☐	15 ☐	21 ☐	☐
5 ☐	11 ☐	17 ☐	23 ☐	☐

KEY CARDS I HAVE: ______________________

OF CARDS I HAVE: ______________________

KEY CARDS I NEED: ______________________

OF CARDS I NEED: ______________________

COMMENTS: ______________________

% OF SET FILLED: ______________________

13 Card Set

1972 AUBURN TIGERS (COLLEGE)

1C ☐	4C ☐	7C ☐	10C ☐	13C ☐
1D ☐	4D ☐	7D ☐	10D ☐	13D ☐
1H ☐	4H ☐	7H ☐	10H ☐	13H ☐
1S ☐	4S ☐	7S ☐	10S ☐	13S ☐
2C ☐	5C ☐	8C ☐	11C ☐	JK ☐
2D ☐	5D ☐	8D ☐	11D ☐	JK ☐
2H ☐	5H ☐	8H ☐	11H ☐	☐
2S ☐	5S ☐	8S ☐	11S ☐	☐
3C ☐	6C ☐	9C ☐	12C ☐	☐
3D ☐	6D ☐	9D ☐	12D ☐	☐
3H ☐	6H ☐	9H ☐	12H ☐	☐
3S ☐	6S ☐	9S ☐	12S ☐	☐

KEY CARDS I HAVE: ____________________

OF CARDS I HAVE: ____________________

KEY CARDS I NEED: ____________________

OF CARDS I NEED: ____________________

COMMENTS: ____________________

% OF SET FILLED: ____________________

54 Card Set

1972 COWBOYS TEAM ISSUE (NFL)

☐	☐	☐	☐	☐
☐	☐	☐	☐	☐
☐	☐	☐	☐	☐

KEY CARDS I HAVE: ____________________

OF CARDS I HAVE: ____________________

KEY CARDS I NEED: ____________________

OF CARDS I NEED: ____________________

COMMENTS: ____________________

% OF SET FILLED: ____________________

13 Card Set

1972 FLEER QUIZ (NFL)

1 ☐ 7 ☐ 13 ☐ 19 ☐ 25 ☐
2 ☐ 8 ☐ 14 ☐ 20 ☐ 26 ☐
3 ☐ 9 ☐ 15 ☐ 21 ☐ 27 ☐
4 ☐ 10 ☐ 16 ☐ 22 ☐ 28 ☐
5 ☐ 11 ☐ 17 ☐ 23 ☐ ☐
6 ☐ 12 ☐ 18 ☐ 24 ☐ ☐

KEY CARDS I HAVE:

KEY CARDS I NEED:

OF CARDS I HAVE:

COMMENTS:

OF CARDS I NEED:

% OF SET FILLED:

28 Card Set

1972 49ERS REDWOOD CITY TRIBUTE (NFL)

☐ ☐ ☐ ☐
☐ ☐ ☐ ☐

KEY CARDS I HAVE:

KEY CARDS I NEED:

OF CARDS I HAVE:

COMMENTS:

OF CARDS I NEED:

% OF SET FILLED:

6 Card Set

1972 NFLPA

1972 NFLPA IRON ONS (NFL)

KEY CARDS I HAVE:

KEY CARDS I NEED:

COMMENTS:

OF CARDS I HAVE:

OF CARDS I NEED:

% OF SET FILLED:

35 Card Set

1972 NFLPA VINYL STICKERS (NFL)

KEY CARDS I HAVE:

KEY CARDS I NEED:

COMMENTS:

OF CARDS I HAVE:

OF CARDS I NEED:

% OF SET FILLED:

20 Card Set

1972 NFLPA WONDERFUL WORLD STAMPS (NFL)

1	51	101	151	201	251	301	351
2	52	102	152	202	252	302	352
3	53	103	153	203	253	303	353
4	54	104	154	204	254	304	354
5	55	105	155	205	255	305	355
6	56	106	156	206	256	306	356
7	57	107	157	207	257	307	357
8	58	108	158	208	258	308	358
9	59	109	159	209	259	39	359
10	60	110	160	210	260	310	360
11	61	111	161	211	261	311	361
12	62	112	162	212	262	312	362
13	63	113	163	213	263	313	363
14	64	114	164	214	264	314	364
15	65	115	165	215	265	315	365
16	66	116	166	216	266	316	366
17	67	117	167	217	267	317	367
18	68	118	168	218	268	318	368
19	69	119	169	219	269	319	369
20	70	120	170	220	270	320	370
21	71	121	171	221	271	321	371
22	72	122	172	222	272	322	372
23	73	123	173	223	273	323	373
24	74	124	174	224	274	324	374
25	75	125	175	225	275	325	375
26	76	126	176	226	276	326	376
27	77	127	177	227	277	327	377
28	78	128	178	228	278	328	378
29	79	129	179	229	279	329	379
30	80	130	180	230	280	330	380
31	81	131	181	231	281	331	381
32	82	132	182	232	282	332	382
33	83	133	183	233	283	333	383
34	84	134	184	234	284	334	384
35	85	135	185	235	285	335	385
36	86	136	186	236	286	336	386
37	87	137	187	237	287	337	387
38	88	138	188	238	288	338	388
39	89	139	189	239	289	339	389
40	90	140	190	240	290	340	390
41	91	141	191	241	291	341	
42	92	142	192	242	292	342	
43	93	143	193	243	293	343	
44	94	144	194	244	294	344	
45	95	145	195	245	295	345	
46	96	146	196	246	296	346	
47	97	147	197	247	297	347	
48	98	148	198	248	298	348	
49	99	149	199	249	299	349	
50	100	150	200	250	300	350	

OF CARDS I HAVE: ____________

OF CARDS I NEED: ____________

% OF SET FILLED: ____________

KEY CARDS I HAVE:

KEY CARDS I NEED:

COMMENTS:

1972 O-PEE-CHEE (CFL)

1 ☐	26 ☐	51 ☐	76 ☐	101 ☐	126 ☐
2 ☐	27 ☐	52 ☐	77 ☐	102 ☐	127 ☐
3 ☐	28 ☐	53 ☐	78 ☐	103 ☐	128 ☐
4 ☐	29 ☐	54 ☐	79 ☐	104 ☐	129 ☐
5 ☐	30 ☐	55 ☐	80 ☐	105 ☐	130 ☐
6 ☐	31 ☐	56 ☐	81 ☐	106 ☐	131 ☐
7 ☐	32 ☐	57 ☐	82 ☐	107 ☐	132 ☐
8 ☐	33 ☐	58 ☐	83 ☐	108 ☐	☐
9 ☐	34 ☐	59 ☐	84 ☐	109 ☐	☐
10 ☐	35 ☐	60 ☐	85 ☐	110 ☐	☐
11 ☐	36 ☐	61 ☐	86 ☐	111 ☐	☐
12 ☐	37 ☐	62 ☐	87 ☐	112 ☐	☐
13 ☐	38 ☐	63 ☐	88 ☐	113 ☐	☐
14 ☐	39 ☐	64 ☐	89 ☐	114 ☐	☐
15 ☐	40 ☐	65 ☐	90 ☐	115 ☐	☐
16 ☐	41 ☐	66 ☐	91 ☐	116 ☐	☐
17 ☐	42 ☐	67 ☐	92 ☐	117 ☐	☐
18 ☐	43 ☐	68 ☐	93 ☐	118 ☐	☐
19 ☐	44 ☐	69 ☐	94 ☐	119 ☐	☐
20 ☐	45 ☐	70 ☐	95 ☐	120 ☐	☐
21 ☐	46 ☐	71 ☐	96 ☐	121 ☐	☐
22 ☐	47 ☐	72 ☐	97 ☐	122 ☐	☐
23 ☐	48 ☐	73 ☐	98 ☐	123 ☐	☐
24 ☐	49 ☐	74 ☐	99 ☐	124 ☐	☐
25 ☐	50 ☐	75 ☐	100 ☐	125 ☐	☐

BLUE BOMBERS

OF CARDS I HAVE: ____________

OF CARDS I NEED: ____________

% OF SET FILLED: ____________

KEY CARDS I HAVE:

KEY CARDS I NEED:

COMMENTS:

1972 O-PEE-CHEE CFL TRIO STICKER INSERT (CFL)

1 ☐	16 ☐	31 ☐	46 ☐	61 ☐
4 ☐	19 ☐	34 ☐	49 ☐	64 ☐
7 ☐	22 ☐	37 ☐	52 ☐	67 ☐
10 ☐	25 ☐	40 ☐	55 ☐	70 ☐
13 ☐	28 ☐	43 ☐	58 ☐	☐

KEY CARDS I HAVE: ____________________

KEY CARDS I NEED: ____________________

COMMENTS: ____________________

\# OF CARDS I HAVE: ____________

\# OF CARDS I NEED: ____________

% OF SET FILLED: ____________

24 Card Set

1972 OILERS TEAM ISSUE (NFL)

☐	☐	☐	☐
☐	☐	☐	☐
☐	☐	☐	☐
☐	☐	☐	☐

KEY CARDS I HAVE: ____________________

KEY CARDS I NEED: ____________________

COMMENTS: ____________________

\# OF CARDS I HAVE: ____________

\# OF CARDS I NEED: ____________

% OF SET FILLED: ____________

11 Card Set

1972 PACKERS TEAM ISSUE (NFL)

1 ☐	11 ☐	21 ☐	31 ☐	41 ☐
2 ☐	12 ☐	22 ☐	32 ☐	42 ☐
3 ☐	13 ☐	23 ☐	33 ☐	43 ☐
4 ☐	14 ☐	24 ☐	34 ☐	44 ☐
5 ☐	15 ☐	25 ☐	35 ☐	45 ☐
6 ☐	16 ☐	26 ☐	36 ☐	☐
7 ☐	17 ☐	27 ☐	37 ☐	☐
8 ☐	18 ☐	28 ☐	38 ☐	☐
9 ☐	19 ☐	29 ☐	39 ☐	☐
10 ☐	20 ☐	30 ☐	40 ☐	☐

KEY CARDS I HAVE: # OF CARDS I HAVE:

KEY CARDS I NEED: # OF CARDS I NEED:

COMMENTS: % OF SET FILLED:

45 Card Set

1972 REDSKINS CARICATURE (NFL)

☐	☐	☐	☐
☐	☐	☐	☐
☐	☐	☐	☐
☐	☐	☐	☐
☐	☐	☐	☐

KEY CARDS I HAVE: # OF CARDS I HAVE:

KEY CARDS I NEED: # OF CARDS I NEED:

COMMENTS: % OF SET FILLED:

16 Card Set

1972 7-11 SLURPEE CUPS (NFL)

1 ☐	13 ☐	25 ☐	37 ☐	49 ☐	☐
2 ☐	14 ☐	26 ☐	38 ☐	50 ☐	☐
3 ☐	15 ☐	27 ☐	39 ☐	51 ☐	☐
4 ☐	16 ☐	28 ☐	40 ☐	52 ☐	☐
5 ☐	17 ☐	29 ☐	41 ☐	53 ☐	☐
6 ☐	18 ☐	30 ☐	42 ☐	54 ☐	☐
7 ☐	19 ☐	31 ☐	43 ☐	55 ☐	☐
8 ☐	20 ☐	32 ☐	44 ☐	56 ☐	☐
9 ☐	21 ☐	33 ☐	45 ☐	57 ☐	☐
10 ☐	22 ☐	34 ☐	46 ☐	58 ☐	☐
11 ☐	23 ☐	35 ☐	47 ☐	59 ☐	☐
12 ☐	24 ☐	36 ☐	48 ☐	60 ☐	☐

KEY CARDS I HAVE: ____________________

KEY CARDS I NEED: ____________________

COMMENTS: ____________________

OF CARDS I HAVE: ________

OF CARDS I NEED: ________

% OF SET FILLED: ________

60 Card Set

1972 STEELERS PHOTO SHEETS (NFL)

1 ☐	4 ☐	7 ☐	☐
2 ☐	5 ☐	8 ☐	☐
3 ☐	6 ☐	☐	☐

KEY CARDS I HAVE: ____________________

KEY CARDS I NEED: ____________________

COMMENTS: ____________________

OF CARDS I HAVE: ________

OF CARDS I NEED: ________

% OF SET FILLED: ________

8 Card Set

1972 Sunoco Stamps (NFL)

13 Don Maynard WR
New York Jets

\# of cards I have:

\# of cards I need:

% of set filled:

Key Cards I Have:

Key Cards I Need:

Comments:

1972 SUNOCO STAMPS UPDATE (NFL)

81 Marv Bateman P
Dallas Cowboys

NEW PLAYER

OF CARDS I HAVE:

OF CARDS I NEED:

% OF SET FILLED:

KEY CARDS I HAVE:

KEY CARDS I NEED:

COMMENTS:

1972 Topps (NFL)

1 ☐	51 ☐	101 ☐	151 ☐	201 ☐	251 ☐	301 ☐
2 ☐	52 ☐	102 ☐	152 ☐	202 ☐	252 ☐	302 ☐
3 ☐	53 ☐	103 ☐	153 ☐	203 ☐	253 ☐	303 ☐
4 ☐	54 ☐	104 ☐	154 ☐	204 ☐	254 ☐	304 ☐
5 ☐	55 ☐	105 ☐	155 ☐	205 ☐	255 ☐	305 ☐
6 ☐	56 ☐	106 ☐	156 ☐	206 ☐	256 ☐	306 ☐
7 ☐	57 ☐	107 ☐	157 ☐	207 ☐	257 ☐	307 ☐
8 ☐	58 ☐	108 ☐	158 ☐	208 ☐	258 ☐	308 ☐
9 ☐	59 ☐	109 ☐	159 ☐	209 ☐	259 ☐	39 ☐
10 ☐	60 ☐	110 ☐	160 ☐	210 ☐	260 ☐	310 ☐
11 ☐	61 ☐	111 ☐	161 ☐	211 ☐	261 ☐	311 ☐
12 ☐	62 ☐	112 ☐	162 ☐	212 ☐	262 ☐	312 ☐
13 ☐	63 ☐	113 ☐	163 ☐	213 ☐	263 ☐	313 ☐
14 ☐	64 ☐	114 ☐	164 ☐	214 ☐	264 ☐	314 ☐
15 ☐	65 ☐	115 ☐	165 ☐	215 ☐	265 ☐	315 ☐
16 ☐	66 ☐	116 ☐	166 ☐	216 ☐	266 ☐	316 ☐
17 ☐	67 ☐	117 ☐	167 ☐	217 ☐	267 ☐	317 ☐
18 ☐	68 ☐	118 ☐	168 ☐	218 ☐	268 ☐	318 ☐
19 ☐	69 ☐	119 ☐	169 ☐	219 ☐	269 ☐	319 ☐
20 ☐	70 ☐	120 ☐	170 ☐	220 ☐	270 ☐	320 ☐
21 ☐	71 ☐	121 ☐	171 ☐	221 ☐	271 ☐	321 ☐
22 ☐	72 ☐	122 ☐	172 ☐	222 ☐	272 ☐	322 ☐
23 ☐	73 ☐	123 ☐	173 ☐	223 ☐	273 ☐	323 ☐
24 ☐	74 ☐	124 ☐	174 ☐	224 ☐	274 ☐	324 ☐
25 ☐	75 ☐	125 ☐	175 ☐	225 ☐	275 ☐	325 ☐
26 ☐	76 ☐	126 ☐	176 ☐	226 ☐	276 ☐	326 ☐
27 ☐	77 ☐	127 ☐	177 ☐	227 ☐	277 ☐	327 ☐
28 ☐	78 ☐	128 ☐	178 ☐	228 ☐	278 ☐	328 ☐
29 ☐	79 ☐	129 ☐	179 ☐	229 ☐	279 ☐	329 ☐
30 ☐	80 ☐	130 ☐	180 ☐	230 ☐	280 ☐	330 ☐
31 ☐	81 ☐	131 ☐	181 ☐	231 ☐	281 ☐	331 ☐
32 ☐	82 ☐	132 ☐	182 ☐	232 ☐	282 ☐	332 ☐
33 ☐	83 ☐	133 ☐	183 ☐	233 ☐	283 ☐	333 ☐
34 ☐	84 ☐	134 ☐	184 ☐	234 ☐	284 ☐	334 ☐
35 ☐	85 ☐	135 ☐	185 ☐	235 ☐	285 ☐	335 ☐
36 ☐	86 ☐	136 ☐	186 ☐	236 ☐	286 ☐	336 ☐
37 ☐	87 ☐	137 ☐	187 ☐	237 ☐	287 ☐	337 ☐
38 ☐	88 ☐	138 ☐	188 ☐	238 ☐	288 ☐	338 ☐
39 ☐	89 ☐	139 ☐	189 ☐	239 ☐	289 ☐	339 ☐
40 ☐	90 ☐	140 ☐	190 ☐	240 ☐	290 ☐	340 ☐
41 ☐	91 ☐	141 ☐	191 ☐	241 ☐	291 ☐	341 ☐
42 ☐	92 ☐	142 ☐	192 ☐	242 ☐	292 ☐	342 ☐
43 ☐	93 ☐	143 ☐	193 ☐	243 ☐	293 ☐	343 ☐
44 ☐	94 ☐	144 ☐	194 ☐	244 ☐	294 ☐	344 ☐
45 ☐	95 ☐	145 ☐	195 ☐	245 ☐	295 ☐	345 ☐
46 ☐	96 ☐	146 ☐	196 ☐	246 ☐	296 ☐	346 ☐
47 ☐	97 ☐	147 ☐	197 ☐	247 ☐	297 ☐	347 ☐
48 ☐	98 ☐	148 ☐	198 ☐	248 ☐	298 ☐	348 ☐
49 ☐	99 ☐	149 ☐	199 ☐	249 ☐	299 ☐	349 ☐
50 ☐	100 ☐	150 ☐	200 ☐	250 ☐	300 ☐	350 ☐

351 ☐

OF CARDS I HAVE: ____________

OF CARDS I NEED: ____________

% OF SET FILLED: ____________

KEY CARDS I HAVE: ____________

KEY CARDS I NEED: ____________

COMMENTS: ____________

1973

1973 AUBURN TIGERS (COLLEGE)

1C ☐	4C ☐	7C ☐	10C ☐	13C ☐
1D ☐	4D ☐	7D ☐	10D ☐	13D ☐
1H ☐	4H ☐	7H ☐	10H ☐	13H ☐
1S ☐	4S ☐	7S ☐	10S ☐	13S ☐
2C ☐	5C ☐	8C ☐	11C ☐	JK ☐
2D ☐	5D ☐	8D ☐	11D ☐	JK ☐
2H ☐	5H ☐	8H ☐	11H ☐	☐
2S ☐	5S ☐	8S ☐	11S ☐	☐
3C ☐	6C ☐	9C ☐	12C ☐	☐
3D ☐	6D ☐	9D ☐	12D ☐	☐
3H ☐	6H ☐	9H ☐	12H ☐	☐
3S ☐	6S ☐	9S ☐	12S ☐	☐

KEY CARDS I HAVE: ______________________

OF CARDS I HAVE: ______

KEY CARDS I NEED: ______________________

OF CARDS I NEED: ______

COMMENTS: ______________________

% OF SET FILLED: ______

54 Card Set

1973 FLEER PRO BOWL SCOUTING REPORT (NFL)

☐	☐	☐	☐	☐
☐	☐	☐	☐	☐
☐	☐	☐	☐	☐
☐	☐	☐	☐	☐

KEY CARDS I HAVE: ______________________

OF CARDS I HAVE: ______

KEY CARDS I NEED: ______________________

OF CARDS I NEED: ______

COMMENTS: ______________________

% OF SET FILLED: ______

14 Card Set

NOTES

NOTES

1973 COLORADO STATE (COLLEGE)

1 ☐ 4 ☐ 7 ☐ ☐
2 ☐ 5 ☐ 8 ☐ ☐
3 ☐ 6 ☐ ☐ ☐

OF CARDS I HAVE: ______

OF CARDS I NEED: ______

% OF SET FILLED: ______

KEY CARDS I HAVE: ______

KEY CARDS I NEED: ______

COMMENTS: ______

8 Card Set

1973 GIANTS COLOR LITHO (NFL)

☐ ☐ ☐ ☐
☐ ☐ ☐ ☐
☐ ☐ ☐ ☐

OF CARDS I HAVE: ______

OF CARDS I NEED: ______

% OF SET FILLED: ______

KEY CARDS I HAVE: ______

KEY CARDS I NEED: ______

COMMENTS: ______

8 Card Set

1973 WASHINGTON KFC (COLLEGE)

1 ☐ 8 ☐ 15 ☐ 22 ☐ 29 ☐
2 ☐ 9 ☐ 16 ☐ 23 ☐ 30 ☐
3 ☐ 10 ☐ 17 ☐ 24 ☐ ☐
4 ☐ 11 ☐ 18 ☐ 25 ☐ ☐
5 ☐ 12 ☐ 19 ☐ 26 ☐ ☐
6 ☐ 13 ☐ 20 ☐ 27 ☐ ☐
7 ☐ 14 ☐ 21 ☐ 28 ☐ ☐

OF CARDS I HAVE: ______

OF CARDS I NEED: ______

% OF SET FILLED: ______

KEY CARDS I HAVE: ______

KEY CARDS I NEED: ______

COMMENTS: ______

30 Card Set

1973 OILERS TEAM ISSUE (NFL)

KEY CARDS I HAVE:

KEY CARDS I NEED:

COMMENTS:

OF CARDS I HAVE:

OF CARDS I NEED:

% OF SET FILLED:

17 Card Set

1973 OILERS MCDONALDS (NFL)

KEY CARDS I HAVE:

KEY CARDS I NEED:

COMMENTS:

OF CARDS I HAVE:

OF CARDS I NEED:

% OF SET FILLED:

3 Card Set

1973 RAMS TEAM ISSUE (NFL)

KEY CARDS I HAVE:

KEY CARDS I NEED:

COMMENTS:

OF CARDS I HAVE:

OF CARDS I NEED:

% OF SET FILLED:

6 Card Set

1973 7-11 SLURPEE CUPS (NFL)

1 ☐	16 ☐	31 ☐	46 ☐	61 ☐	76 ☐
2 ☐	17 ☐	32 ☐	47 ☐	62 ☐	77 ☐
3 ☐	18 ☐	33 ☐	48 ☐	63 ☐	78 ☐
4 ☐	19 ☐	34 ☐	49 ☐	64 ☐	79 ☐
5 ☐	20 ☐	35 ☐	50 ☐	65 ☐	80 ☐
6 ☐	21 ☐	36 ☐	51 ☐	66 ☐	☐
7 ☐	22 ☐	37 ☐	52 ☐	67 ☐	☐
8 ☐	23 ☐	38 ☐	53 ☐	68 ☐	☐
9 ☐	24 ☐	39 ☐	54 ☐	69 ☐	☐
10 ☐	25 ☐	40 ☐	55 ☐	70 ☐	☐
11 ☐	26 ☐	41 ☐	56 ☐	71 ☐	☐
12 ☐	27 ☐	42 ☐	57 ☐	72 ☐	☐
13 ☐	28 ☐	43 ☐	58 ☐	73 ☐	☐
14 ☐	29 ☐	44 ☐	59 ☐	74 ☐	☐
15 ☐	30 ☐	45 ☐	60 ☐	75 ☐	☐

OF CARDS I HAVE: ____________

OF CARDS I NEED: ____________

% OF SET FILLED: ____________

KEY CARDS I HAVE: ____________

KEY CARDS I NEED: ____________

COMMENTS: ____________

1973 Topps (NFL)

1	51	101	151	201	251	301	351	401	451	501
2	52	102	152	202	252	302	352	402	452	502
3	53	103	153	203	253	303	353	403	453	503
4	54	104	154	204	254	304	354	404	454	504
5	55	105	155	205	255	305	355	405	455	505
6	56	106	156	206	256	306	356	406	456	506
7	57	107	157	207	257	307	357	407	457	507
8	58	108	158	208	258	308	358	408	458	508
9	59	109	159	209	259	39	359	409	459	509
10	60	110	160	210	260	310	360	410	460	510
11	61	111	161	211	261	311	361	411	461	511
12	62	112	162	212	262	312	362	412	462	512
13	63	113	163	213	263	313	363	413	463	513
14	64	114	164	214	264	314	364	414	464	514
15	65	115	165	215	265	315	365	415	465	515
16	66	116	166	216	266	316	366	416	466	516
17	67	117	167	217	267	317	367	417	437	517
18	68	118	168	218	268	318	368	418	468	518
19	69	119	169	219	269	319	369	419	469	519
20	70	120	170	220	270	320	370	420	470	520
21	71	121	171	221	271	321	371	421	471	521
22	72	122	172	222	272	322	372	422	472	522
23	73	123	173	223	273	323	373	423	473	523
24	74	124	174	224	274	324	374	424	474	524
25	75	125	175	225	275	325	375	425	475	525
26	76	126	176	226	276	326	376	426	476	526
27	77	127	177	227	277	327	377	427	477	527
28	78	128	178	228	278	328	378	428	478	528
29	79	129	179	229	279	329	379	429	479	
30	80	130	180	230	280	330	380	430	480	
31	81	131	181	231	281	331	381	431	481	
32	82	132	182	232	282	332	382	432	482	
33	83	133	183	233	283	333	383	433	483	
34	84	134	184	234	284	334	384	434	484	
35	85	135	185	235	285	335	385	435	485	
36	86	136	186	236	286	336	386	436	486	
37	87	137	187	237	287	337	387	437	487	
38	88	138	188	238	288	338	388	438	488	
39	89	139	189	239	289	339	389	439	489	
40	90	140	190	240	290	340	390	440	490	
41	91	141	191	241	291	341	391	441	491	
42	92	142	192	242	292	342	392	442	492	
43	93	143	193	243	293	343	393	443	493	
44	94	144	194	244	294	344	394	444	494	
45	95	145	195	245	295	345	395	445	495	
46	96	146	196	246	296	346	396	446	496	
47	97	147	197	247	297	347	397	447	497	
48	98	148	198	248	298	348	398	448	498	
49	99	149	199	249	299	349	399	449	499	
50	100	150	200	250	300	350	400	450	500	

EUGENE UPSHAW
GUARD
RAIDERS

OF CARDS I HAVE:

OF CARDS I NEED:

% OF SET FILLED:

KEY CARDS I HAVE:

KEY CARDS I NEED:

COMMENTS:

1973 ALABAMA TEAM SHEETS (COLLEGE)

1C	4C	7C	10C	13C
1D	4D	7D	10D	13D
1H	4H	7H	10H	13H
1S	4S	7S	10S	13S
2C	5C	8C	11C	JK
2D	5D	8D	11D	JK
2H	5H	8H	11H	
2S	5S	8S	11S	
3C	6C	9C	12C	
3D	6D	9D	12D	
3H	6H	9H	12H	
3S	6S	9S	12S	

KEY CARDS I HAVE:

OF CARDS I HAVE:

KEY CARDS I NEED:

OF CARDS I NEED:

COMMENTS:

% OF SET FILLED:

54 Card Set

1973 - 74 CHIEFS TEAM ISSUE (NFL)

1	5	9	13	17
2	6	10	14	18
3	7	11	15	
4	8	12	16	

KEY CARDS I HAVE:

OF CARDS I HAVE:

KEY CARDS I NEED:

OF CARDS I NEED:

COMMENTS:

% OF SET FILLED:

18 Card Set

1973-74 TOPPS TEAM CHECKLISTS

1973 TOPPS TEAM CHECKLISTS (NFL)

1 ☐	6 ☐	11 ☐	16 ☐	21 ☐	26 ☐
2 ☐	7 ☐	12 ☐	17 ☐	22 ☐	☐
3 ☐	8 ☐	13 ☐	18 ☐	23 ☐	☐
4 ☐	9 ☐	14 ☐	19 ☐	24 ☐	☐
5 ☐	10 ☐	15 ☐	20 ☐	25 ☐	☐

KEY CARDS I HAVE: ______

KEY CARDS I NEED: ______

COMMENTS: ______

OF CARDS I HAVE: ______

OF CARDS I NEED: ______

% OF SET FILLED: ______

26 Card Set

1974 TOPPS TEAM CHECKLISTS (NFL)

☐	☐	☐	☐	☐	☐
☐	☐	☐	☐	☐	☐
☐	☐	☐	☐	☐	☐
☐	☐	☐	☐	☐	☐
☐	☐	☐	☐	☐	☐

KEY CARDS I HAVE: ______

KEY CARDS I NEED: ______

COMMENTS: ______

OF CARDS I HAVE: ______

OF CARDS I NEED: ______

% OF SET FILLED: ______

26 Card Set

1974

1974 BILLS TEAM ISSUE (NFL)

1 ☐ 4 ☐ 7 ☐ 10 ☐ ☐
2 ☐ 5 ☐ 8 ☐ 11 ☐ ☐
3 ☐ 6 ☐ 9 ☐ 12 ☐ ☐

OF CARDS I HAVE: ____________

KEY CARDS I HAVE: ____________

OF CARDS I NEED: ____________

KEY CARDS I NEED: ____________

COMMENTS: ____________

% OF SET FILLED: ____________

12 Card Set

1974 DOLPHINS ALL-PRO GRAPHICS (NFL)

☐ ☐ ☐ ☐
☐ ☐ ☐ ☐
☐ ☐ ☐ ☐

OF CARDS I HAVE: ____________

KEY CARDS I HAVE: ____________

OF CARDS I NEED: ____________

KEY CARDS I NEED: ____________

COMMENTS: ____________

% OF SET FILLED: ____________

10 Card Set

1974 PACKERS TEAM ISSUE (NFL)

1 ☐ 6 ☐ 11 ☐ ☐
2 ☐ 7 ☐ 12 ☐ ☐
3 ☐ 8 ☐ 13 ☐ ☐
4 ☐ 9 ☐ 14 ☐ ☐
5 ☐ 10 ☐ ☐ ☐

OF CARDS I HAVE: ____________

KEY CARDS I HAVE: ____________

OF CARDS I NEED: ____________

KEY CARDS I NEED: ____________

COMMENTS: ____________

% OF SET FILLED: ____________

14 Card Set

1974 FLEER

1974 FLEER BIG SIGNS (NFL)

KEY CARDS I HAVE:

KEY CARDS I NEED:

COMMENTS:

OF CARDS I HAVE:

OF CARDS I NEED:

% OF SET FILLED:

26 Card Set

1974 FLEER HALL OF FAME (NFL)

KEY CARDS I HAVE:

KEY CARDS I NEED:

COMMENTS:

OF CARDS I HAVE:

OF CARDS I NEED:

% OF SET FILLED:

50 Card Set

1974 NEBRASKA (COLLEGE)

1 ☐	11 ☐	21 ☐	31 ☐	41 ☐	51 ☐
2 ☐	12 ☐	22 ☐	32 ☐	42 ☐	52 ☐
3 ☐	13 ☐	23 ☐	33 ☐	43 ☐	53 ☐
4 ☐	14 ☐	24 ☐	34 ☐	44 ☐	54 ☐
5 ☐	15 ☐	25 ☐	35 ☐	45 ☐	☐
6 ☐	16 ☐	26 ☐	36 ☐	46 ☐	☐
7 ☐	17 ☐	27 ☐	37 ☐	47 ☐	☐
8 ☐	18 ☐	28 ☐	38 ☐	48 ☐	☐
9 ☐	19 ☐	29 ☐	39 ☐	49 ☐	☐
10 ☐	20 ☐	30 ☐	40 ☐	50 ☐	☐

OF CARDS I HAVE: ____________

KEY CARDS I HAVE: ____

____

OF CARDS I NEED: ____________

KEY CARDS I NEED: ____

____

% OF SET FILLED: ____________

COMMENTS: ____

54 Card Set

1974 PARKERS BROTHERS PRO DRAFT (NFL)

4 ☐	23 ☐	46 ☐	65 ☐	95 ☐	116 ☐
6 ☐	24 ☐	49 ☐	75 ☐	98 ☐	119 ☐
7 ☐	28 ☐	50 ☐	77 ☐	101 ☐	124 ☐
9 ☐	32 ☐	52 ☐	78 ☐	103 ☐	126 ☐
11 ☐	35 ☐	54 ☐	80 ☐	107 ☐	127 ☐
15 ☐	39 ☐	57 ☐	81 ☐	109 ☐	☐
18 ☐	42 ☐	58 ☐	83 ☐	110 ☐	☐
19 ☐	43 ☐	61 ☐	87 ☐	111 ☐	☐
21 ☐	44 ☐	63 ☐	90 ☐	113 ☐	☐

OF CARDS I HAVE: ____________

KEY CARDS I HAVE: ____

____

OF CARDS I NEED: ____________

KEY CARDS I NEED: ____

____

% OF SET FILLED: ____________

COMMENTS: ____

50 Card Set

1974 SAINTS CIRCLE INSET (NFL)

KEY CARDS I HAVE:

KEY CARDS I NEED:

COMMENTS:

OF CARDS I HAVE:

OF CARDS I NEED:

% OF SET FILLED:

22 Card Set

1974 SOUTHERN CAL DISCS (COLLEGE)

1	8	15	22	29
2	9	16	23	30
3	10	17	24	
4	11	18	25	
5	12	19	26	
6	13	20	27	
7	14	21	28	

KEY CARDS I HAVE:

KEY CARDS I NEED:

COMMENTS:

OF CARDS I HAVE:

OF CARDS I NEED:

% OF SET FILLED:

30 Card Set

1974 WEST VIRGINIA (COLLEGE)

1C ☐	3H ☐	6C ☐	8H ☐	11C ☐	13H ☐
1D ☐	3S ☐	6D ☐	8S ☐	11D ☐	13S ☐
1H ☐	4C ☐	6H ☐	9C ☐	11H ☐	JK ☐
1S ☐	4D ☐	6S ☐	9D ☐	11S ☐	☐
2C ☐	4H ☐	7C ☐	9H ☐	12C ☐	☐
2D ☐	4S ☐	7D ☐	9S ☐	12D ☐	☐
2H ☐	5C ☐	7H ☐	10C ☐	12H ☐	☐
2S ☐	5D ☐	7S ☐	10D ☐	12S ☐	☐
3C ☐	5H ☐	8C ☐	10H ☐	13C ☐	☐
3D ☐	5S ☐	8D ☐	10S ☐	13D ☐	☐

KEY CARDS I HAVE: ______________________

KEY CARDS I NEED: ______________________

COMMENTS: ______________________

OF CARDS I HAVE: __________

OF CARDS I NEED: __________

% OF SET FILLED: __________

53 Card Set

1974 WONDER BREAD (NFL)

1 ☐	8 ☐	15 ☐	22 ☐	29 ☐
2 ☐	9 ☐	16 ☐	23 ☐	30 ☐
3 ☐	10 ☐	17 ☐	24 ☐	☐
4 ☐	11 ☐	18 ☐	25 ☐	☐
5 ☐	12 ☐	19 ☐	26 ☐	☐
6 ☐	13 ☐	20 ☐	27 ☐	☐
7 ☐	14 ☐	21 ☐	28 ☐	☐

KEY CARDS I HAVE: ______________________

KEY CARDS I NEED: ______________________

COMMENTS: ______________________

OF CARDS I HAVE: __________

OF CARDS I NEED: __________

% OF SET FILLED: __________

30 Card Set

1974 Topps (NFL)

1 ☐	51 ☐	101 ☐	151 ☐	201 ☐	251 ☐	301 ☐	351 ☐	401 ☐	451 ☐	501 ☐
2 ☐	52 ☐	102 ☐	152 ☐	202 ☐	252 ☐	302 ☐	352 ☐	402 ☐	452 ☐	502 ☐
3 ☐	53 ☐	103 ☐	153 ☐	203 ☐	253 ☐	303 ☐	353 ☐	403 ☐	453 ☐	503 ☐
4 ☐	54 ☐	104 ☐	154 ☐	204 ☐	254 ☐	304 ☐	354 ☐	404 ☐	454 ☐	504 ☐
5 ☐	55 ☐	105 ☐	155 ☐	205 ☐	255 ☐	305 ☐	355 ☐	405 ☐	455 ☐	505 ☐
6 ☐	56 ☐	106 ☐	156 ☐	206 ☐	256 ☐	306 ☐	356 ☐	406 ☐	456 ☐	506 ☐
7 ☐	57 ☐	107 ☐	157 ☐	207 ☐	257 ☐	307 ☐	357 ☐	407 ☐	457 ☐	507 ☐
8 ☐	58 ☐	108 ☐	158 ☐	208 ☐	258 ☐	308 ☐	358 ☐	408 ☐	458 ☐	508 ☐
9 ☐	59 ☐	109 ☐	159 ☐	209 ☐	259 ☐	39 ☐	359 ☐	409 ☐	459 ☐	509 ☐
10 ☐	60 ☐	110 ☐	160 ☐	210 ☐	260 ☐	310 ☐	360 ☐	410 ☐	460 ☐	510 ☐
11 ☐	61 ☐	111 ☐	161 ☐	211 ☐	261 ☐	311 ☐	361 ☐	411 ☐	461 ☐	511 ☐
12 ☐	62 ☐	112 ☐	162 ☐	212 ☐	262 ☐	312 ☐	362 ☐	412 ☐	462 ☐	512 ☐
13 ☐	63 ☐	113 ☐	163 ☐	213 ☐	263 ☐	313 ☐	363 ☐	413 ☐	463 ☐	513 ☐
14 ☐	64 ☐	114 ☐	164 ☐	214 ☐	264 ☐	314 ☐	364 ☐	414 ☐	464 ☐	514 ☐
15 ☐	65 ☐	115 ☐	165 ☐	215 ☐	265 ☐	315 ☐	365 ☐	415 ☐	465 ☐	515 ☐
16 ☐	66 ☐	116 ☐	166 ☐	216 ☐	266 ☐	316 ☐	366 ☐	416 ☐	466 ☐	516 ☐
17 ☐	67 ☐	117 ☐	167 ☐	217 ☐	267 ☐	317 ☐	367 ☐	417 ☐	437 ☐	517 ☐
18 ☐	68 ☐	118 ☐	168 ☐	218 ☐	268 ☐	318 ☐	368 ☐	418 ☐	468 ☐	518 ☐
19 ☐	69 ☐	119 ☐	169 ☐	219 ☐	269 ☐	319 ☐	369 ☐	419 ☐	469 ☐	519 ☐
20 ☐	70 ☐	120 ☐	170 ☐	220 ☐	270 ☐	320 ☐	370 ☐	420 ☐	470 ☐	520 ☐
21 ☐	71 ☐	121 ☐	171 ☐	221 ☐	271 ☐	321 ☐	371 ☐	421 ☐	471 ☐	521 ☐
22 ☐	72 ☐	122 ☐	172 ☐	222 ☐	272 ☐	322 ☐	372 ☐	422 ☐	472 ☐	522 ☐
23 ☐	73 ☐	123 ☐	173 ☐	223 ☐	273 ☐	323 ☐	373 ☐	423 ☐	473 ☐	523 ☐
24 ☐	74 ☐	124 ☐	174 ☐	224 ☐	274 ☐	324 ☐	374 ☐	424 ☐	474 ☐	524 ☐
25 ☐	75 ☐	125 ☐	175 ☐	225 ☐	275 ☐	325 ☐	375 ☐	425 ☐	475 ☐	525 ☐
26 ☐	76 ☐	126 ☐	176 ☐	226 ☐	276 ☐	326 ☐	376 ☐	426 ☐	476 ☐	526 ☐
27 ☐	77 ☐	127 ☐	177 ☐	227 ☐	277 ☐	327 ☐	377 ☐	427 ☐	477 ☐	527 ☐
28 ☐	78 ☐	128 ☐	178 ☐	228 ☐	278 ☐	328 ☐	378 ☐	428 ☐	478 ☐	528 ☐
29 ☐	79 ☐	129 ☐	179 ☐	229 ☐	279 ☐	329 ☐	379 ☐	429 ☐	479 ☐	☐
30 ☐	80 ☐	130 ☐	180 ☐	230 ☐	280 ☐	330 ☐	380 ☐	430 ☐	480 ☐	☐
31 ☐	81 ☐	131 ☐	181 ☐	231 ☐	281 ☐	331 ☐	381 ☐	431 ☐	481 ☐	☐
32 ☐	82 ☐	132 ☐	182 ☐	232 ☐	282 ☐	332 ☐	382 ☐	432 ☐	482 ☐	☐
33 ☐	83 ☐	133 ☐	183 ☐	233 ☐	283 ☐	333 ☐	383 ☐	433 ☐	483 ☐	☐
34 ☐	84 ☐	134 ☐	184 ☐	234 ☐	284 ☐	334 ☐	384 ☐	434 ☐	484 ☐	☐
35 ☐	85 ☐	135 ☐	185 ☐	235 ☐	285 ☐	335 ☐	385 ☐	435 ☐	485 ☐	☐
36 ☐	86 ☐	136 ☐	186 ☐	236 ☐	286 ☐	336 ☐	386 ☐	436 ☐	486 ☐	☐
37 ☐	87 ☐	137 ☐	187 ☐	237 ☐	287 ☐	337 ☐	387 ☐	437 ☐	487 ☐	☐
38 ☐	88 ☐	138 ☐	188 ☐	238 ☐	288 ☐	338 ☐	388 ☐	438 ☐	488 ☐	☐
39 ☐	89 ☐	139 ☐	189 ☐	239 ☐	289 ☐	339 ☐	389 ☐	439 ☐	489 ☐	☐
40 ☐	90 ☐	140 ☐	190 ☐	240 ☐	290 ☐	340 ☐	390 ☐	440 ☐	490 ☐	☐
41 ☐	91 ☐	141 ☐	191 ☐	241 ☐	291 ☐	341 ☐	391 ☐	441 ☐	491 ☐	☐
42 ☐	92 ☐	142 ☐	192 ☐	242 ☐	292 ☐	342 ☐	392 ☐	442 ☐	492 ☐	☐
43 ☐	93 ☐	143 ☐	193 ☐	243 ☐	293 ☐	343 ☐	393 ☐	443 ☐	493 ☐	☐
44 ☐	94 ☐	144 ☐	194 ☐	244 ☐	294 ☐	344 ☐	394 ☐	444 ☐	494 ☐	☐
45 ☐	95 ☐	145 ☐	195 ☐	245 ☐	295 ☐	345 ☐	395 ☐	445 ☐	495 ☐	☐
46 ☐	96 ☐	146 ☐	196 ☐	246 ☐	296 ☐	346 ☐	396 ☐	446 ☐	496 ☐	☐
47 ☐	97 ☐	147 ☐	197 ☐	247 ☐	297 ☐	347 ☐	397 ☐	447 ☐	497 ☐	☐
48 ☐	98 ☐	148 ☐	198 ☐	248 ☐	298 ☐	348 ☐	398 ☐	448 ☐	498 ☐	☐
49 ☐	99 ☐	149 ☐	199 ☐	249 ☐	299 ☐	349 ☐	399 ☐	449 ☐	499 ☐	☐
50 ☐	100 ☐	150 ☐	200 ☐	250 ☐	300 ☐	350 ☐	400 ☐	450 ☐	500 ☐	☐

ROGER STAUBACH QUARTERBACK
COWBOYS

OF CARDS I HAVE: ____________

OF CARDS I NEED: ____________

% OF SET FILLED: ____________

KEY CARDS I HAVE: ____________

KEY CARDS I NEED: ____________

COMMENTS: ____________

1975 FLEER HALL OF FAME (NFL)

1 ☐	16 ☐	31 ☐	46 ☐	61 ☐	76 ☐
2 ☐	17 ☐	32 ☐	47 ☐	62 ☐	77 ☐
3 ☐	18 ☐	33 ☐	48 ☐	63 ☐	78 ☐
4 ☐	19 ☐	34 ☐	49 ☐	64 ☐	79 ☐
5 ☐	20 ☐	35 ☐	50 ☐	65 ☐	80 ☐
6 ☐	21 ☐	36 ☐	51 ☐	66 ☐	81 ☐
7 ☐	22 ☐	37 ☐	52 ☐	67 ☐	82 ☐
8 ☐	23 ☐	38 ☐	53 ☐	68 ☐	83 ☐
9 ☐	24 ☐	39 ☐	54 ☐	69 ☐	84 ☐
10 ☐	25 ☐	40 ☐	55 ☐	70 ☐	☐
11 ☐	26 ☐	41 ☐	56 ☐	71 ☐	☐
12 ☐	27 ☐	42 ☐	57 ☐	72 ☐	☐
13 ☐	28 ☐	43 ☐	58 ☐	73 ☐	☐
14 ☐	29 ☐	44 ☐	59 ☐	74 ☐	☐
15 ☐	30 ☐	45 ☐	60 ☐	75 ☐	☐

OF CARDS I HAVE: ____________

OF CARDS I NEED: ____________

% OF SET FILLED: ____________

KEY CARDS I HAVE: ____________

KEY CARDS I NEED: ____________

COMMENTS: ____________

1975

1975 LAUGHLIN FLAKY (NFL)

1 ☐	7 ☐	13 ☐	19 ☐	25 ☐
2 ☐	8 ☐	14 ☐	20 ☐	26 ☐
3 ☐	9 ☐	15 ☐	21 ☐	27 ☐
4 ☐	10 ☐	16 ☐	22 ☐	☐
5 ☐	11 ☐	17 ☐	23 ☐	☐
6 ☐	12 ☐	18 ☐	24 ☐	☐

KEY CARDS I HAVE: ______________________

OF CARDS I HAVE: ______________

KEY CARDS I NEED: ______________________

OF CARDS I NEED: ______________

COMMENTS: ______________________

% OF SET FILLED: ______________

27 Card Set

1975 MCDONALDS QUARTERBACKS (NFL)

☐ ☐ ☐ ☐ ☐

KEY CARDS I HAVE: ______________________

OF CARDS I HAVE: ______________

KEY CARDS I NEED: ______________________

OF CARDS I NEED: ______________

COMMENTS: ______________________

% OF SET FILLED: ______________

4 Card Set

1975 TOPPS TEAM CHECKLIST (NFL)

KEY CARDS I HAVE:

KEY CARDS I NEED:

COMMENTS:

OF CARDS I HAVE:

OF CARDS I NEED:

% OF SET FILLED:

26 Card Set

1975 WONDER BREAD (NFL)

1	7	13	19
2	8	14	20
3	9	15	21
4	10	16	22
5	11	17	23
6	12	18	24

KEY CARDS I HAVE:

KEY CARDS I NEED:

COMMENTS:

OF CARDS I HAVE:

OF CARDS I NEED:

% OF SET FILLED:

24 Card Set

1975 Topps (NFL)

1	51	101	151	201	251	301	351	401	451	501
2	52	102	152	202	252	302	352	402	452	502
3	53	103	153	203	253	303	353	403	453	503
4	54	104	154	204	254	304	354	404	454	504
5	55	105	155	205	255	305	355	405	455	505
6	56	106	156	206	256	306	356	406	456	506
7	57	107	157	207	257	307	357	407	457	507
8	58	108	158	208	258	308	358	408	458	508
9	59	109	159	209	259	39	359	409	459	509
10	60	110	160	210	260	310	360	410	460	510
11	61	111	161	211	261	311	361	411	461	511
12	62	112	162	212	262	312	362	412	462	512
13	63	113	163	213	263	313	363	413	463	513
14	64	114	164	214	264	314	364	414	464	514
15	65	115	165	215	265	315	365	415	465	515
16	66	116	166	216	266	316	366	416	466	516
17	67	117	167	217	267	317	367	417	437	517
18	68	118	168	218	268	318	368	418	468	518
19	69	119	169	219	269	319	369	419	469	519
20	70	120	170	220	270	320	370	420	470	520
21	71	121	171	221	271	321	371	421	471	521
22	72	122	172	222	272	322	372	422	472	522
23	73	123	173	223	273	323	373	423	473	523
24	74	124	174	224	274	324	374	424	474	524
25	75	125	175	225	275	325	375	425	475	525
26	76	126	176	226	276	326	376	426	476	526
27	77	127	177	227	277	327	377	427	477	527
28	78	128	178	228	278	328	378	428	478	528
29	79	129	179	229	279	329	379	429	479	
30	80	130	180	230	280	330	380	430	480	
31	81	131	181	231	281	331	381	431	481	
32	82	132	182	232	282	332	382	432	482	
33	83	133	183	233	283	333	383	433	483	
34	84	134	184	234	284	334	384	434	484	
35	85	135	185	235	285	335	385	435	485	
36	86	136	186	236	286	336	386	436	486	
37	87	137	187	237	287	337	387	437	487	
38	88	138	188	238	288	338	388	438	488	
39	89	139	189	239	289	339	389	439	489	
40	90	140	190	240	290	340	390	440	490	
41	91	141	191	241	291	341	391	441	491	
42	92	142	192	242	292	342	392	442	492	
43	93	143	193	243	293	343	393	443	493	
44	94	144	194	244	294	344	394	444	494	
45	95	145	195	245	295	345	395	445	495	
46	96	146	196	246	296	346	396	446	496	
47	97	147	197	247	297	347	397	447	497	
48	98	148	198	248	298	348	398	448	498	
49	99	149	199	249	299	349	399	449	499	
50	100	150	200	250	300	350	400	450	500	

PATRIOTS AFC GUARD
JOHN HANNAH

OF CARDS I HAVE:

OF CARDS I NEED:

% OF SET FILLED:

KEY CARDS I HAVE:

KEY CARDS I NEED:

COMMENTS:

1976

1976 BEARS COKE DISCS (NFL)

1 ☐	6B ☐	12 ☐	17 ☐	☐
2 ☐	7 ☐	13 ☐	18 ☐	☐
3 ☐	8 ☐	14 ☐	19 ☐	☐
4 ☐	9 ☐	15 ☐	20 ☐	☐
5 ☐	10 ☐	16A ☐	21 ☐	☐
6A ☐	11 ☐	16B ☐	22 ☐	☐

KEY CARDS I HAVE: ______

KEY CARDS I NEED: ______

COMMENTS: ______

OF CARDS I HAVE: ______

OF CARDS I NEED: ______

% OF SET FILLED: ______

24 Card Set

1976 BUCKMAN DISCS (NFL)

☐	☐	☐	☐	☐
☐	☐	☐	☐	☐
☐	☐	☐	☐	☐
☐	☐	☐	☐	☐
☐	☐	☐	☐	☐

KEY CARDS I HAVE: ______

KEY CARDS I NEED: ______

COMMENTS: ______

OF CARDS I HAVE: ______

OF CARDS I NEED: ______

% OF SET FILLED: ______

20 Card Set

1976 BILLS MCDONALDS (NFL)

1 ☐ 2 ☐ 3 ☐ ☐

KEY CARDS I HAVE: ______

KEY CARDS I NEED: ______

COMMENTS: ______

OF CARDS I HAVE: ______

OF CARDS I NEED: ______

% OF SET FILLED: ______

3 Card Set

1976 FLEER TEAM ACTION (NFL)

1 ☐	16 ☐	31 ☐	46 ☐	61 ☐
2 ☐	17 ☐	32 ☐	47 ☐	62 ☐
3 ☐	18 ☐	33 ☐	48 ☐	63 ☐
4 ☐	19 ☐	34 ☐	49 ☐	64 ☐
5 ☐	20 ☐	35 ☐	50 ☐	65 ☐
6 ☐	21 ☐	36 ☐	51 ☐	66 ☐
7 ☐	22 ☐	37 ☐	52 ☐	☐
8 ☐	23 ☐	38 ☐	53 ☐	☐
9 ☐	24 ☐	39 ☐	54 ☐	☐
10 ☐	25 ☐	40 ☐	55 ☐	☐
11 ☐	26 ☐	41 ☐	56 ☐	☐
12 ☐	27 ☐	42 ☐	57 ☐	☐
13 ☐	28 ☐	43 ☐	58 ☐	☐
14 ☐	29 ☐	44 ☐	59 ☐	☐
15 ☐	30 ☐	45 ☐	60 ☐	☐

TAMPA BAY BUCCANEERS • STADIUM

OF CARDS I HAVE: ____________

OF CARDS I NEED: ____________

% OF SET FILLED: ____________

KEY CARDS I HAVE:

KEY CARDS I NEED:

COMMENTS:

1976 CRANE DISCS (NFL)

KEY CARDS I HAVE:

KEY CARDS I NEED:

COMMENTS:

OF CARDS I HAVE:

OF CARDS I NEED:

% OF SET FILLED:

30 Card Set

1976 CHARGERS DEANS PHOTOS (NFL)

1
2
3
4
5
6
7
8
9
10

KEY CARDS I HAVE:

KEY CARDS I NEED:

COMMENTS:

OF CARDS I HAVE:

OF CARDS I NEED:

% OF SET FILLED:

10 Card Set

1976 NALLEYS CHIPS (CFL)

1	9	17	25	
2	10	18	26	
3	11	19	27	
4	12	20	28	
5	13	21	29	
6	14	22	30	
7	15	23		
8	16	24		

KEY CARDS I HAVE:

KEY CARDS I NEED:

COMMENTS:

OF CARDS I HAVE:

OF CARDS I NEED:

% OF SET FILLED:

30 Card Set

1976 PEPSI DISCS (NFL)

1	11	21	31	
2	12	22	32	
3	13	23	33	
4	14	24	34	
5	15	25	35	
6	16	26	36	
7	17	27	37	
8	18	28	38	
9	19	29	39	
10	20	30	40	

KEY CARDS I HAVE:

KEY CARDS I NEED:

COMMENTS:

OF CARDS I HAVE:

OF CARDS I NEED:

% OF SET FILLED:

40 Card Set

1976 POPSICLE TEAMS (NFL)

KEY CARDS I HAVE:

KEY CARDS I NEED:

COMMENTS:

OF CARDS I HAVE:

OF CARDS I NEED:

% OF SET FILLED:

30 Card Set

1976 SAGA DISCS (NFL)

1
2
3
4
5
6
7
8
9
10
11
12
13
14
15
16
17
18
19
20
21
22
23
24
25
26
27
28
29
30

KEY CARDS I HAVE:

KEY CARDS I NEED:

COMMENTS:

OF CARDS I HAVE:

OF CARDS I NEED:

% OF SET FILLED:

30 Card Set

1976 SUNBEAM

1976 SUNBEAM NFL DIE CUTS (NFL)

1 ☐	8 ☐	15 ☐	22 ☐	☐
2 ☐	9 ☐	16 ☐	23 ☐	☐
3 ☐	10 ☐	17 ☐	24 ☐	☐
4 ☐	11 ☐	18 ☐	25 ☐	☐
5 ☐	12 ☐	19 ☐	26 ☐	☐
6 ☐	13 ☐	20 ☐	27 ☐	☐
7 ☐	14 ☐	21 ☐	28 ☐	☐

KEY CARDS I HAVE: ______________________

KEY CARDS I NEED: ______________________

COMMENTS: ______________________

OF CARDS I HAVE: ______________

OF CARDS I NEED: ______________

% OF SET FILLED: ______________

29 Card Set

1976 SUNBEAM SEC DIE CUTS (COLLEGE)

1 ☐	6 ☐	11 ☐	16 ☐	☐
2 ☐	7 ☐	12 ☐	17 ☐	☐
3 ☐	8 ☐	13 ☐	18 ☐	☐
4 ☐	9 ☐	14 ☐	19 ☐	☐
5 ☐	10 ☐	15 ☐	20 ☐	☐

KEY CARDS I HAVE: ______________________

KEY CARDS I NEED: ______________________

COMMENTS: ______________________

OF CARDS I HAVE: ______________

OF CARDS I NEED: ______________

% OF SET FILLED: ______________

20 Card Set

1976 CONT. 4

1976 TOPPS TEAM CHECKLISTS (NFL)

DALLAS COWBOYS
CHECK LIST

Card#	Player	Pos.	Unif.#
102	Fitzgerald, John	C	62
132	Fritsch, Toni	K	15
447	Fugett, Jean	TE	84
260	Harris, Cliff	S	43
283	Hoopes, Mitch	P	9
427	Jones, "Too Tall"	DE	72
490	Jordan, Lee Roy	MLB	55
342	Lewis, D.D.	LB	50
44	Martin, Harvey	DE	79
14	Newhouse, Robert	RB	44
527	Nye, Blaine	G	61
313	Pearson, Drew	WR	88
225	Pearson, Preston	RB	26
368	Renfro, Mel	CB	20
73	Richards, Golden	WR	83
395	Staubach, Roger	QB	12
457	TEAM CARD		
158	White, Randy	LB	54
190	Wright, Rayfield	T	70

KEY CARDS I HAVE:

\# OF CARDS I HAVE:

KEY CARDS I NEED:

\# OF CARDS I NEED:

COMMENTS:

% OF SET FILLED:

30 Card Set

1976 WONDER BREAD (NFL)

1 2 3 4 5 6 7
8 9 10 11 12 13 14
15 16 17 18 19 20 21
22 23 24

JACK TATUM
SAFETY
RAIDERS-A.F.C.

KEY CARDS I HAVE:

\# OF CARDS I HAVE:

KEY CARDS I NEED:

\# OF CARDS I NEED:

COMMENTS:

% OF SET FILLED:

24 Card Set

1976 Topps (NFL)

1	51	101	151	201	251	301	351	401	451	501
2	52	102	152	202	252	302	352	402	452	502
3	53	103	153	203	253	303	353	403	453	503
4	54	104	154	204	254	304	354	404	454	504
5	55	105	155	205	255	305	355	405	455	505
6	56	106	156	206	256	306	356	406	456	506
7	57	107	157	207	257	307	357	407	457	507
8	58	108	158	208	258	308	358	408	458	508
9	59	109	159	209	259	309	359	409	459	509
10	60	110	160	210	260	310	360	410	460	510
11	61	111	161	211	261	311	361	411	461	511
12	62	112	162	212	262	312	362	412	462	512
13	63	113	163	213	263	313	363	413	463	513
14	64	114	164	214	264	314	364	414	464	514
15	65	115	165	215	265	315	365	415	465	515
16	66	116	166	216	266	316	366	416	466	516
17	67	117	167	217	267	317	367	417	437	517
18	68	118	168	218	268	318	368	418	468	518
19	69	119	169	219	269	319	369	419	469	519
20	70	120	170	220	270	320	370	420	470	520
21	71	121	171	221	271	321	371	421	471	521
22	72	122	172	222	272	322	372	422	472	522
23	73	123	173	223	273	323	373	423	473	523
24	74	124	174	224	274	324	374	424	474	524
25	75	125	175	225	275	325	375	425	475	525
26	76	126	176	226	276	326	376	426	476	526
27	77	127	177	227	277	327	377	427	477	527
28	78	128	178	228	278	328	378	428	478	528
29	79	129	179	229	279	329	379	429	479	
30	80	130	180	230	280	330	380	430	480	
31	81	131	181	231	281	331	381	431	481	
32	82	132	182	232	282	332	382	432	482	
33	83	133	183	233	283	333	383	433	483	
34	84	134	184	234	284	334	384	434	484	
35	85	135	185	235	285	335	385	435	485	
36	86	136	186	236	286	336	386	436	486	
37	87	137	187	237	287	337	387	437	487	
38	88	138	188	238	288	338	388	438	488	
39	89	139	189	239	289	339	389	439	489	
40	90	140	190	240	290	340	390	440	490	
41	91	141	191	241	291	341	391	441	491	
42	92	142	192	242	292	342	392	442	492	
43	93	143	193	243	293	343	393	443	493	
44	94	144	194	244	294	344	394	444	494	
45	95	145	195	245	295	345	395	445	495	
46	96	146	196	246	296	346	396	446	496	
47	97	147	197	247	297	347	397	447	497	
48	98	148	198	248	298	348	398	448	498	
49	99	149	199	249	299	349	399	449	499	
50	100	150	200	250	300	350	400	450	500	

BEARS
RUNNING BACK
WALTER PAYTON

OF CARDS I HAVE:

OF CARDS I NEED:

% OF SET FILLED:

KEY CARDS I HAVE:

KEY CARDS I NEED:

COMMENTS:

1977 FLEER TEAM ACTION (NFL)

1 ☐	16 ☐	31 ☐	46 ☐	61 ☐
2 ☐	17 ☐	32 ☐	47 ☐	62 ☐
3 ☐	18 ☐	33 ☐	48 ☐	63 ☐
4 ☐	19 ☐	34 ☐	49 ☐	64 ☐
5 ☐	20 ☐	35 ☐	50 ☐	65 ☐
6 ☐	21 ☐	36 ☐	51 ☐	66 ☐
7 ☐	22 ☐	37 ☐	52 ☐	67 ☐
8 ☐	23 ☐	38 ☐	53 ☐	☐
9 ☐	24 ☐	39 ☐	54 ☐	☐
10 ☐	25 ☐	40 ☐	55 ☐	☐
11 ☐	26 ☐	41 ☐	56 ☐	☐
12 ☐	27 ☐	42 ☐	57 ☐	☐
13 ☐	28 ☐	43 ☐	58 ☐	☐
14 ☐	29 ☐	44 ☐	59 ☐	☐
15 ☐	30 ☐	45 ☐	60 ☐	☐

DALLAS COWBOYS
UNASSISTED SACK

OF CARDS I HAVE: ______

OF CARDS I NEED: ______

% OF SET FILLED: ______

KEY CARDS I HAVE:

KEY CARDS I NEED:

COMMENTS:

1977

1977 MARKETCOM TEST (NFL)

☐ ☐ ☐ ☐

KEY CARDS I HAVE:

KEY CARDS I NEED:

COMMENTS:

OF CARDS I HAVE:

OF CARDS I NEED:

% OF SET FILLED:

2 Card Set

1977 NEBRASKA (COLLEGE)

1 ☐	13 ☐	25 ☐	37 ☐	49 ☐
2 ☐	14 ☐	26 ☐	38 ☐	50 ☐
3 ☐	15 ☐	27 ☐	39 ☐	51 ☐
4 ☐	16 ☐	28 ☐	40 ☐	52 ☐
5 ☐	17 ☐	29 ☐	41 ☐	53 ☐
6 ☐	18 ☐	30 ☐	42 ☐	54 ☐
7 ☐	19 ☐	31 ☐	43 ☐	☐
8 ☐	20 ☐	32 ☐	44 ☐	☐
9 ☐	21 ☐	33 ☐	45 ☐	☐
10 ☐	22 ☐	34 ☐	46 ☐	☐
11 ☐	23 ☐	35 ☐	47 ☐	☐
12 ☐	24 ☐	36 ☐	48 ☐	☐

KEY CARDS I HAVE:

KEY CARDS I NEED:

COMMENTS:

OF CARDS I HAVE:

OF CARDS I NEED:

% OF SET FILLED:

54 Card Set

NOTES

NOTES

1977 MICHIGAN (COLLEGE)

1☐ 6☐ 11☐ 16☐ 21☐
2☐ 7☐ 12☐ 17☐ ☐
3☐ 8☐ 13☐ 18☐ ☐
4☐ 9☐ 14☐ 19☐ ☐
5☐ 10☐ 15☐ 20☐ ☐

KEY CARDS I HAVE: ____________________

KEY CARDS I NEED: ____________________

COMMENTS: ____________________

OF CARDS I HAVE: ____________

OF CARDS I NEED: ____________

% OF SET FILLED: ____________

21 Card Set

1977 POTTSVILLE MAROONS (NFL)

1☐ 5☐ 9☐ 13☐ 17☐
2☐ 6☐ 10☐ 14☐ ☐
3☐ 7☐ 11☐ 15☐ ☐
4☐ 8☐ 12☐ 16☐ ☐

KEY CARDS I HAVE: ____________________

KEY CARDS I NEED: ____________________

COMMENTS: ____________________

OF CARDS I HAVE: ____________

OF CARDS I NEED: ____________

% OF SET FILLED: ____________

17 Card Set

1977 CONT. 2

1977 SEAHAWKS TEAM ISSUE (NFL)

1 ☐ 4 ☐ 7 ☐ 10 ☐
2 ☐ 5 ☐ 8 ☐ ☐
3 ☐ 6 ☐ 9 ☐ ☐

OF CARDS I HAVE: ______

KEY CARDS I HAVE: ______

OF CARDS I NEED: ______

KEY CARDS I NEED: ______

COMMENTS: ______

% OF SET FILLED: ______

10 Card Set

1977 SEAHAWKS FRED MEYER (NFL)

1 ☐ 5 ☐ 9 ☐ 13A ☐
2 ☐ 6 ☐ 10 ☐ 13B ☐
3 ☐ 7 ☐ 11 ☐ ☐
4 ☐ 8 ☐ 12 ☐ ☐

OF CARDS I HAVE: ______

KEY CARDS I HAVE: ______

OF CARDS I NEED: ______

KEY CARDS I NEED: ______

COMMENTS: ______

% OF SET FILLED: ______

14 Card Set

1977 TOPPS HOLSUM PACKERS/VIKINGS (NFL)

1 ☐ 6 ☐ 11 ☐ 16 ☐ 21 ☐
2 ☐ 7 ☐ 12 ☐ 17 ☐ 22 ☐
3 ☐ 8 ☐ 13 ☐ 18 ☐ ☐
4 ☐ 9 ☐ 14 ☐ 19 ☐ ☐
5 ☐ 10 ☐ 15 ☐ 20 ☐ ☐

OF CARDS I HAVE: ______

KEY CARDS I HAVE: ______

KEY CARDS I NEED: ______

OF CARDS I NEED: ______

COMMENTS: ______

% OF SET FILLED: ______

22 Card Set

1977 Topps (NFL)

1	51	101	151	201	251	301	351	401	451	501
2	52	102	152	202	252	302	352	402	452	502
3	53	103	153	203	253	303	353	403	453	503
4	54	104	154	204	254	304	354	404	454	504
5	55	105	155	205	255	305	355	405	455	505
6	56	106	156	206	256	306	356	406	456	506
7	57	107	157	207	257	307	357	407	457	507
8	58	108	158	208	258	308	358	408	458	508
9	59	109	159	209	259	39	359	409	459	509
10	60	110	160	210	260	310	360	410	460	510
11	61	111	161	211	261	311	361	411	461	511
12	62	112	162	212	262	312	362	412	462	512
13	63	113	163	213	263	313	363	413	463	513
14	64	114	164	214	264	314	364	414	464	514
15	65	115	165	215	265	315	365	415	465	515
16	66	116	166	216	266	316	366	416	466	516
17	67	117	167	217	267	317	367	417	437	517
18	68	118	168	218	268	318	368	418	468	518
19	69	119	169	219	269	319	369	419	469	519
20	70	120	170	220	270	320	370	420	470	520
21	71	121	171	221	271	321	371	421	471	521
22	72	122	172	222	272	322	372	422	472	522
23	73	123	173	223	273	323	373	423	473	523
24	74	124	174	224	274	324	374	424	474	524
25	75	125	175	225	275	325	375	425	475	525
26	76	126	176	226	276	326	376	426	476	526
27	77	127	177	227	277	327	377	427	477	527
28	78	128	178	228	278	328	378	428	478	528
29	79	129	179	229	279	329	379	429	479	
30	80	130	180	230	280	330	380	430	480	
31	81	131	181	231	281	331	381	431	481	
32	82	132	182	232	282	332	382	432	482	
33	83	133	183	233	283	333	383	433	483	
34	84	134	184	234	284	334	384	434	484	
35	85	135	185	235	285	335	385	435	485	
36	86	136	186	236	286	336	386	436	486	
37	87	137	187	237	287	337	387	437	487	
38	88	138	188	238	288	338	388	438	488	
39	89	139	189	239	289	339	389	439	489	
40	90	140	190	240	290	340	390	440	490	
41	91	141	191	241	291	341	391	441	491	
42	92	142	192	242	292	342	392	442	492	
43	93	143	193	243	293	343	393	443	493	
44	94	144	194	244	294	344	394	444	494	
45	95	145	195	245	295	345	395	445	495	
46	96	146	196	246	296	346	396	446	496	
47	97	147	197	247	297	347	397	447	497	
48	98	148	198	248	298	348	398	448	498	
49	99	149	199	249	299	349	399	449	499	
50	100	150	200	250	300	350	400	450	500	

OF CARDS I HAVE:

OF CARDS I NEED:

% OF SET FILLED:

KEY CARDS I HAVE:

KEY CARDS I NEED:

COMMENTS:

1977 TOPPS INSERTS

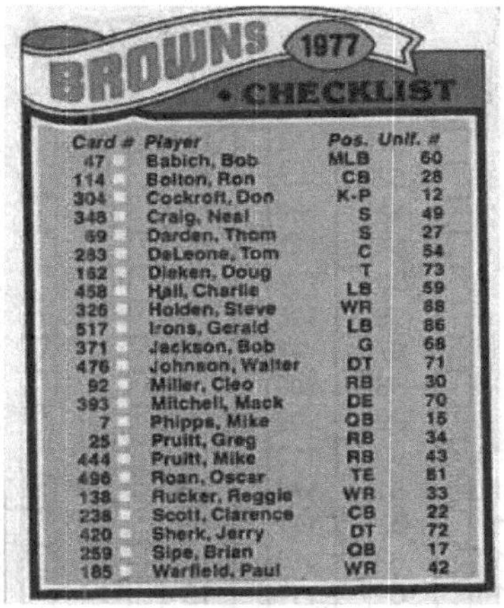

1977 TOPPS TEAM CHECKLISTS (NFL)

1 ☐	9 ☐	17 ☐	25 ☐	☐
2 ☐	10 ☐	18 ☐	26 ☐	☐
3 ☐	11 ☐	19 ☐	27 ☐	☐
4 ☐	12 ☐	20 ☐	28 ☐	☐
5 ☐	13 ☐	21 ☐	NN01 ☐	☐
6 ☐	14 ☐	22 ☐	NN02 ☐	☐
7 ☐	15 ☐	23 ☐	☐	☐
8 ☐	16 ☐	24 ☐	☐	☐

KEY CARDS I HAVE: __________

KEY CARDS I NEED: __________

COMMENTS: __________

OF CARDS I HAVE: __________

OF CARDS I NEED: __________

% OF SET FILLED: __________

30 Card Set

1977 TOPPS TOUCHDOWN CLUB (NFL)

1 ☐	11 ☐	21 ☐	31 ☐	41 ☐	☐
2 ☐	12 ☐	22 ☐	32 ☐	42 ☐	☐
3 ☐	13 ☐	23 ☐	33 ☐	43 ☐	☐
4 ☐	14 ☐	24 ☐	34 ☐	44 ☐	☐
5 ☐	15 ☐	25 ☐	35 ☐	45 ☐	☐
6 ☐	16 ☐	26 ☐	36 ☐	46 ☐	☐
7 ☐	17 ☐	27 ☐	37 ☐	47 ☐	☐
8 ☐	18 ☐	28 ☐	38 ☐	48 ☐	☐
9 ☐	19 ☐	29 ☐	39 ☐	49 ☐	☐
10 ☐	20 ☐	30 ☐	40 ☐	50 ☐	☐

KEY CARDS I HAVE: __________

KEY CARDS I NEED: __________

COMMENTS: __________

OF CARDS I HAVE: __________

OF CARDS I NEED: __________

% OF SET FILLED: __________

50 Card Set

1977 Topps Mexican (NFL)

1	51	101	151	201	251	301	351	401	451	501
2	52	102	152	202	252	302	352	402	452	502
3	53	103	153	203	253	303	353	403	453	503
4	54	104	154	204	254	304	354	404	454	504
5	55	105	155	205	255	305	355	405	455	505
6	56	106	156	206	256	306	356	406	456	506
7	57	107	157	207	257	307	357	407	457	507
8	58	108	158	208	258	308	358	408	458	508
9	59	109	159	209	259	39	359	409	459	509
10	60	110	160	210	260	310	360	410	460	510
11	61	111	161	211	261	311	361	411	461	511
12	62	112	162	212	262	312	362	412	462	512
13	63	113	163	213	263	313	363	413	463	513
14	64	114	164	214	264	314	364	414	464	514
15	65	115	165	215	265	315	365	415	465	515
16	66	116	166	216	266	316	366	416	466	516
17	67	117	167	217	267	317	367	417	437	517
18	68	118	168	218	268	318	368	418	468	518
19	69	119	169	219	269	319	369	419	469	519
20	70	120	170	220	270	320	370	420	470	520
21	71	121	171	221	271	321	371	421	471	521
22	72	122	172	222	272	322	372	422	472	522
23	73	123	173	223	273	323	373	423	473	523
24	74	124	174	224	274	324	374	424	474	524
25	75	125	175	225	275	325	375	425	475	525
26	76	126	176	226	276	326	376	426	476	526
27	77	127	177	227	277	327	377	427	477	527
28	78	128	178	228	278	328	378	428	478	528
29	79	129	179	229	279	329	379	429	479	
30	80	130	180	230	280	330	380	430	480	
31	81	131	181	231	281	331	381	431	481	
32	82	132	182	232	282	332	382	432	482	
33	83	133	183	233	283	333	383	433	483	
34	84	134	184	234	284	334	384	434	484	
35	85	135	185	235	285	335	385	435	485	
36	86	136	186	236	286	336	386	436	486	
37	87	137	187	237	287	337	387	437	487	
38	88	138	188	238	288	338	388	438	488	
39	89	139	189	239	289	339	389	439	489	
40	90	140	190	240	290	340	390	440	490	
41	91	141	191	241	291	341	391	441	491	
42	92	142	192	242	292	342	392	442	492	
43	93	143	193	243	293	343	393	443	493	
44	94	144	194	244	294	344	394	444	494	
45	95	145	195	245	295	345	395	445	495	
46	96	146	196	246	296	346	396	446	496	
47	97	147	197	247	297	347	397	447	497	
48	98	148	198	248	298	348	398	448	498	
49	99	149	199	249	299	349	399	449	499	
50	100	150	200	250	300	350	400	450	500	

OF CARDS I HAVE:

OF CARDS I NEED:

% OF SET FILLED:

KEY CARDS I HAVE:

KEY CARDS I NEED:

COMMENTS:

1978

1978 COLTS TEAM ISSUE (NFL)

KEY CARDS I HAVE:

KEY CARDS I NEED:

COMMENTS:

OF CARDS I HAVE:

OF CARDS I NEED:

% OF SET FILLED:

28 Card Set

1978 FALCONS KINNET DAIRIES (NFL)

KEY CARDS I HAVE:

KEY CARDS I NEED:

COMMENTS:

OF CARDS I HAVE:

OF CARDS I NEED:

% OF SET FILLED:

6 Card Set

1978 FLEER TEAM ACTION (NFL)

1 ☐	16 ☐	31 ☐	46 ☐	61 ☐
2 ☐	17 ☐	32 ☐	47 ☐	62 ☐
3 ☐	18 ☐	33 ☐	48 ☐	63 ☐
4 ☐	19 ☐	34 ☐	49 ☐	64 ☐
5 ☐	20 ☐	35 ☐	50 ☐	65 ☐
6 ☐	21 ☐	36 ☐	51 ☐	66 ☐
7 ☐	22 ☐	37 ☐	52 ☐	67 ☐
8 ☐	23 ☐	38 ☐	53 ☐	68 ☐
9 ☐	24 ☐	39 ☐	54 ☐	☐
10 ☐	25 ☐	40 ☐	55 ☐	☐
11 ☐	26 ☐	41 ☐	56 ☐	☐
12 ☐	27 ☐	42 ☐	57 ☐	☐
13 ☐	28 ☐	43 ☐	58 ☐	☐
14 ☐	29 ☐	44 ☐	59 ☐	☐
15 ☐	30 ☐	45 ☐	60 ☐	☐

OF CARDS I HAVE: ____________

OF CARDS I NEED: ____________

% OF SET FILLED: ____________

KEY CARDS I HAVE:

KEY CARDS I NEED:

COMMENTS:

1978 KELLOGG'S STICKERS (NFL)

1 ☐ 9 ☐ 17 ☐ 25 ☐
2 ☐ 10 ☐ 18 ☐ 26 ☐
3 ☐ 11 ☐ 19 ☐ 27 ☐
4 ☐ 12 ☐ 20 ☐ 28 ☐
5 ☐ 13 ☐ 21 ☐
6 ☐ 14 ☐ 22 ☐
7 ☐ 15 ☐ 23 ☐
8 ☐ 16 ☐ 24 ☐

BALTIMORE COLTS

KEY CARDS I HAVE: ______

KEY CARDS I NEED: ______

COMMENTS: ______

OF CARDS I HAVE: ______

OF CARDS I NEED: ______

% OF SET FILLED: ______

28 Card Set

1978 MARKETCOM TEST (NFL)

Randy White

KEY CARDS I HAVE: ______

KEY CARDS I NEED: ______

COMMENTS: ______

OF CARDS I HAVE: ______

OF CARDS I NEED: ______

% OF SET FILLED: ______

32 Card Set

1978 STEELERS TEAM ISSUE (NFL)

KEY CARDS I HAVE:

KEY CARDS I NEED:

COMMENTS:

OF CARDS I HAVE:

OF CARDS I NEED:

% OF SET FILLED:

8 Card Set

1978 - 80 SEAHAWKS NALLEYS (NFL)

1 2 3 4 5 6 7 8 9 10 11 12 13 14 15 16 17 18 19 20 21 22 23 24

KEY CARDS I HAVE:

KEY CARDS I NEED:

COMMENTS:

OF CARDS I HAVE:

OF CARDS I NEED:

% OF SET FILLED:

24 Card Set

1978 SLIM JIM (NFL)

1A ☐	8B ☐	16A ☐	23B ☐	31A ☐
1B ☐	9A ☐	16B ☐	24A ☐	31B ☐
2A ☐	9B ☐	17A ☐	24B ☐	32A ☐
2B ☐	10A ☐	17B ☐	25A ☐	32B ☐
3A ☐	10B ☐	18A ☐	25B ☐	33A ☐
3B ☐	11A ☐	18B ☐	26A ☐	33B ☐
4A ☐	11B ☐	19A ☐	26B ☐	34A ☐
4B ☐	12A ☐	19B ☐	27A ☐	34B ☐
5A ☐	12B ☐	20A ☐	27B ☐	35A ☐
5B ☐	13A ☐	20B ☐	28A ☐	35B ☐
6A ☐	13B ☐	21A ☐	28B ☐	☐
6B ☐	14A ☐	21B ☐	29A ☐	☐
7A ☐	14B ☐	22A ☐	29B ☐	☐
7B ☐	15A ☐	22B ☐	30A ☐	☐
8A ☐	15B ☐	23A ☐	30B ☐	☐

OF CARDS I HAVE: ____________

OF CARDS I NEED: ____________

% OF SET FILLED: ____________

KEY CARDS I HAVE: ____________

KEY CARDS I NEED: ____________

COMMENTS: ____________

1978 TOPPS HOLSUM (NFL)

1 ☐	11 ☐	21 ☐	31 ☐
2 ☐	12 ☐	22 ☐	32 ☐
3 ☐	13 ☐	23 ☐	33 ☐
4 ☐	14 ☐	24 ☐	☐
5 ☐	15 ☐	25 ☐	☐
6 ☐	16 ☐	26 ☐	☐
7 ☐	17 ☐	27 ☐	☐
8 ☐	18 ☐	28 ☐	☐
9 ☐	19 ☐	29 ☐	☐
10 ☐	20 ☐	30 ☐	☐

DE HARVEY MARTIN
COWBOYS

KEY CARDS I HAVE: ____________________

KEY CARDS I NEED: ____________________

COMMENTS: ____________________

OF CARDS I HAVE: __________

OF CARDS I NEED: __________

% OF SET FILLED: __________

33 Card Set

1978 VIKINGS COUNTRY KITCHEN (NFL)

1 ☐	3 ☐	5 ☐	7 ☐	☐
2 ☐	4 ☐	6 ☐	☐	☐

KEY CARDS I HAVE: ____________________

KEY CARDS I NEED: ____________________

COMMENTS: ____________________

OF CARDS I HAVE: __________

OF CARDS I NEED: __________

% OF SET FILLED: __________

7 Card Set

1978 Topps (NFL)

DOUG PLANK
BEARS

1	51	101	151	201	251	301	351	401	451	501
2	52	102	152	202	252	302	352	402	452	502
3	53	103	153	203	253	303	353	403	453	503
4	54	104	154	204	254	304	354	404	454	504
5	55	105	155	205	255	305	355	405	455	505
6	56	106	156	206	256	306	356	406	456	506
7	57	107	157	207	257	307	357	407	457	507
8	58	108	158	208	258	308	358	408	458	508
9	59	109	159	209	259	39	359	409	459	509
10	60	110	160	210	260	310	360	410	460	510
11	61	111	161	211	261	311	361	411	461	511
12	62	112	162	212	262	312	362	412	462	512
13	63	113	163	213	263	313	363	413	463	513
14	64	114	164	214	264	314	364	414	464	514
15	65	115	165	215	265	315	365	415	465	515
16	66	116	166	216	266	316	366	416	466	516
17	67	117	167	217	267	317	367	417	437	517
18	68	118	168	218	268	318	368	418	468	518
19	69	119	169	219	269	319	369	419	469	519
20	70	120	170	220	270	320	370	420	470	520
21	71	121	171	221	271	321	371	421	471	521
22	72	122	172	222	272	322	372	422	472	522
23	73	123	173	223	273	323	373	423	473	523
24	74	124	174	224	274	324	374	424	474	524
25	75	125	175	225	275	325	375	425	475	525
26	76	126	176	226	276	326	376	426	476	526
27	77	127	177	227	277	327	377	427	477	527
28	78	128	178	228	278	328	378	428	478	528
29	79	129	179	229	279	329	379	429	479	
30	80	130	180	230	280	330	380	430	480	
31	81	131	181	231	281	331	381	431	481	
32	82	132	182	232	282	332	382	432	482	
33	83	133	183	233	283	333	383	433	483	
34	84	134	184	234	284	334	384	434	484	
35	85	135	185	235	285	335	385	435	485	
36	86	136	186	236	286	336	386	436	486	
37	87	137	187	237	287	337	387	437	487	
38	88	138	188	238	288	338	388	438	488	
39	89	139	189	239	289	339	389	439	489	
40	90	140	190	240	290	340	390	440	490	
41	91	141	191	241	291	341	391	441	491	
42	92	142	192	242	292	342	392	442	492	
43	93	143	193	243	293	343	393	443	493	
44	94	144	194	244	294	344	394	444	494	
45	95	145	195	245	295	345	395	445	495	
46	96	146	196	246	296	346	396	446	496	
47	97	147	197	247	297	347	397	447	497	
48	98	148	198	248	298	348	398	448	498	
49	99	149	199	249	299	349	399	449	499	
50	100	150	200	250	300	350	400	450	500	

OF CARDS I HAVE:

OF CARDS I NEED:

% OF SET FILLED:

KEY CARDS I HAVE:

KEY CARDS I NEED:

COMMENTS:

1979 BILLS BELLS MARKET (NFL)

1 □ 4 □ 7 □ 10 □ □
2 □ 5 □ 8 □ 11 □ □
3 □ 6 □ 9 □ □ □

OF CARDS I HAVE:

KEY CARDS I HAVE:

OF CARDS I NEED:

KEY CARDS I NEED:

COMMENTS:

% OF SET FILLED:

11 Card Set

1979 CHIEFS POLICE (NFL)

1 □ 4 □ 7 □ 10 □
2 □ 5 □ 8 □ □
3 □ 6 □ 9 □ □

OF CARDS I HAVE:

OF CARDS I NEED:

KEY CARDS I HAVE:

KEY CARDS I NEED:

% OF SET FILLED:

COMMENTS:

10 Card Set

1979 COWBOYS POLICE (NFL)

1 □ 6 □ 11 □ □
2 □ 7 □ 12 □ □
3 □ 8 □ 13 □ □
4 □ 9 □ 14 □ □
5 □ 10 □ 15 □ □

OF CARDS I HAVE:

KEY CARDS I HAVE:

KEY CARDS I NEED:

OF CARDS I NEED:

COMMENTS:

% OF SET FILLED:

15 Card Set

1979 FLEER TEAM ACTION (NFL)

1 ☐	16 ☐	31 ☐	46 ☐	61 ☐
2 ☐	17 ☐	32 ☐	47 ☐	62 ☐
3 ☐	18 ☐	33 ☐	48 ☐	63 ☐
4 ☐	19 ☐	34 ☐	49 ☐	64 ☐
5 ☐	20 ☐	35 ☐	50 ☐	65 ☐
6 ☐	21 ☐	36 ☐	51 ☐	66 ☐
7 ☐	22 ☐	37 ☐	52 ☐	67 ☐
8 ☐	23 ☐	38 ☐	53 ☐	68 ☐
9 ☐	24 ☐	39 ☐	54 ☐	69 ☐
10 ☐	25 ☐	40 ☐	55 ☐	☐
11 ☐	26 ☐	41 ☐	56 ☐	☐
12 ☐	27 ☐	42 ☐	57 ☐	☐
13 ☐	28 ☐	43 ☐	58 ☐	☐
14 ☐	29 ☐	44 ☐	59 ☐	☐
15 ☐	30 ☐	45 ☐	60 ☐	☐

SUPER BOWL IX
PITTSBURGH (AFC) 16, MINNESOTA (NFC) 6

OF CARDS I HAVE: ____________

OF CARDS I NEED: ____________

% OF SET FILLED: ____________

KEY CARDS I HAVE: ____________

KEY CARDS I NEED: ____________

COMMENTS: ____________

1979 NFLPA PENNANT STICKERS (NFL)

1 ☐	13 ☐	25 ☐	37 ☐	49 ☐
2 ☐	14 ☐	26 ☐	38 ☐	50 ☐
3 ☐	15 ☐	27 ☐	39 ☐	☐
4 ☐	16 ☐	28 ☐	40 ☐	☐
5 ☐	17 ☐	29 ☐	41 ☐	☐
6 ☐	18 ☐	30 ☐	42 ☐	☐
7 ☐	19 ☐	31 ☐	43 ☐	☐
8 ☐	20 ☐	32 ☐	44 ☐	☐
9 ☐	21 ☐	33 ☐	45 ☐	☐
10 ☐	22 ☐	34 ☐	46 ☐	☐
11 ☐	23 ☐	35 ☐	47 ☐	☐
12 ☐	24 ☐	36 ☐	48 ☐	☐

KEY CARDS I HAVE: ____________________

KEY CARDS I NEED: ____________________

COMMENTS: ____________________

OF CARDS I HAVE: ____________________

OF CARDS I NEED: ____________________

% OF SET FILLED: ____________________

50 Card Set

1979 NORTH CAROLINA SCHEDULES (COLLEGE)

1 ☐ 2 ☐ 3 ☐ 4 ☐ ☐

KEY CARDS I HAVE: ____________________

KEY CARDS I NEED: ____________________

COMMENTS: ____________________

OF CARDS I HAVE: ____________________

OF CARDS I NEED: ____________________

% OF SET FILLED: ____________________

4 Card Set

1979 OHIO STATE GREATS (COLLEGE)

1 ☐	11 ☐	21 ☐	31 ☐	41 ☐	51 ☐
2 ☐	12 ☐	22 ☐	32 ☐	42 ☐	52 ☐
3 ☐	13 ☐	23 ☐	33 ☐	43 ☐	53 ☐
4 ☐	14 ☐	24 ☐	34 ☐	44 ☐	☐
5 ☐	15 ☐	25 ☐	35 ☐	45 ☐	☐
6 ☐	16 ☐	26 ☐	36 ☐	46 ☐	☐
7 ☐	17 ☐	27 ☐	37 ☐	47 ☐	☐
8 ☐	18 ☐	28 ☐	38 ☐	48 ☐	☐
9 ☐	19 ☐	29 ☐	39 ☐	49 ☐	☐
10 ☐	20 ☐	30 ☐	40 ☐	50 ☐	☐

KEY CARDS I HAVE: ______ # OF CARDS I HAVE: ______

KEY CARDS I NEED: ______ # OF CARDS I NEED: ______

COMMENTS: ______ % OF SET FILLED: ______

53 Card Set

1979 SEAHAWKS POLICE (NFL)

1 ☐	6 ☐	11 ☐	16 ☐	☐
2 ☐	7 ☐	12 ☐	☐	☐
3 ☐	8 ☐	13 ☐	☐	☐
4 ☐	9 ☐	14 ☐	☐	☐
5 ☐	10 ☐	15 ☐	☐	☐

KEY CARDS I HAVE: ______ # OF CARDS I HAVE: ______

KEY CARDS I NEED: ______ # OF CARDS I NEED: ______

COMMENTS: ______ % OF SET FILLED: ______

16 Card Set

1979 SAINTS COKE (NFL)

1 ☐	11 ☐	21 ☐	31 ☐	41 ☐
2 ☐	12 ☐	22 ☐	32 ☐	42 ☐
3 ☐	13 ☐	23 ☐	33 ☐	43 ☐
4 ☐	14 ☐	24 ☐	34 ☐	44 ☐
5 ☐	15 ☐	25 ☐	35 ☐	45 ☐
6 ☐	16 ☐	26 ☐	36 ☐	☐
7 ☐	17 ☐	27 ☐	37 ☐	☐
8 ☐	18 ☐	28 ☐	38 ☐	☐
9 ☐	19 ☐	29 ☐	39 ☐	☐
10 ☐	20 ☐	30 ☐	40 ☐	☐

ARCHIE MANNING

KEY CARDS I HAVE: ____________________

KEY CARDS I NEED: ____________________

COMMENTS: ____________________

OF CARDS I HAVE: __________

OF CARDS I NEED: __________

% OF SET FILLED: __________

45 Card Set

1979 STOP N GO (NFL)

1 ☐	6 ☐	11 ☐	16 ☐	☐
2 ☐	7 ☐	12 ☐	17 ☐	☐
3 ☐	8 ☐	13 ☐	18 ☐	☐
4 ☐	9 ☐	14 ☐	☐	☐
5 ☐	10 ☐	15 ☐	☐	☐

NFL 3-D FOOTBALL STARS
ROBERT NEWHOUSE
DALLAS COWBOYS

KEY CARDS I HAVE: ____________________

KEY CARDS I NEED: ____________________

COMMENTS: ____________________

OF CARDS I HAVE: __________

OF CARDS I NEED: __________

% OF SET FILLED: __________

18 Card Set

1979 Topps (NFL)

1	51	101	151	201	251	301	351	401	451	501
2	52	102	152	202	252	302	352	402	452	502
3	53	103	153	203	253	303	353	403	453	503
4	54	104	154	204	254	304	354	404	454	504
5	55	105	155	205	255	305	355	405	455	505
6	56	106	156	206	256	306	356	406	456	506
7	57	107	157	207	257	307	357	407	457	507
8	58	108	158	208	258	308	358	408	458	508
9	59	109	159	209	259	39	359	409	459	509
10	60	110	160	210	260	310	360	410	460	510
11	61	111	161	211	261	311	361	411	461	511
12	62	112	162	212	262	312	362	412	462	512
13	63	113	163	213	263	313	363	413	463	513
14	64	114	164	214	264	314	364	414	464	514
15	65	115	165	215	265	315	365	415	465	515
16	66	116	166	216	266	316	366	416	466	516
17	67	117	167	217	267	317	367	417	437	517
18	68	118	168	218	268	318	368	418	468	518
19	69	119	169	219	269	319	369	419	469	519
20	70	120	170	220	270	320	370	420	470	520
21	71	121	171	221	271	321	371	421	471	521
22	72	122	172	222	272	322	372	422	472	522
23	73	123	173	223	273	323	373	423	473	523
24	74	124	174	224	274	324	374	424	474	524
25	75	125	175	225	275	325	375	425	475	525
26	76	126	176	226	276	326	376	426	476	526
27	77	127	177	227	277	327	377	427	477	527
28	78	128	178	228	278	328	378	428	478	528
29	79	129	179	229	279	329	379	429	479	
30	80	130	180	230	280	330	380	430	480	
31	81	131	181	231	281	331	381	431	481	
32	82	132	182	232	282	332	382	432	482	
33	83	133	183	233	283	333	383	433	483	
34	84	134	184	234	284	334	384	434	484	
35	85	135	185	235	285	335	385	435	485	
36	86	136	186	236	286	336	386	436	486	
37	87	137	187	237	287	337	387	437	487	
38	88	138	188	238	288	338	388	438	488	
39	89	139	189	239	289	339	389	439	489	
40	90	140	190	240	290	340	390	440	490	
41	91	141	191	241	291	341	391	441	491	
42	92	142	192	242	292	342	392	442	492	
43	93	143	193	243	293	343	393	443	493	
44	94	144	194	244	294	344	394	444	494	
45	95	145	195	245	295	345	395	445	495	
46	96	146	196	246	296	346	396	446	496	
47	97	147	197	247	297	347	397	447	497	
48	98	148	198	248	298	348	398	448	498	
49	99	149	199	249	299	349	399	449	499	
50	100	150	200	250	300	350	400	450	500	

OF CARDS I HAVE: ____________

OF CARDS I NEED: ____________

% OF SET FILLED: ____________

KEY CARDS I HAVE:

KEY CARDS I NEED:

COMMENTS:

NOTES

THE STADIUM EVENTS

Sports Card Checklists

Coming Soon!!!!!

VINTAGE BASEBALL EDITION – Target release December, 08

VINTAGE BASKETBALL EDITION - Target release April, 09

VINTAGE HOCKEY EDITION - Target release December, 09

SPORTS LOVERS – HERE YOU GO!!!

THE STADIUM EVENTS

Sports Card Checklists

A great tool to inventory your card collection for Football, Baseball Basketball, and Hockey. Designed to be user friendly with the Spiral Binder to allow a flat writing surface, sample pictures for quick identification, and the format to track the cards you have and the cards you need to complete each set. At a glance you can see what Key Cards you have and the ones you need.

THE STADIUM EVENTS LLC

Tickets & Transportation to Sporting Events

THE STADIUM EVENTS LLC is a privately owned company, based out of Fraser, Michigan, specializing in Day Trips and affordable Overnight stays to Sporting Events. All packages include a Ticket to the event and Round Trip Transportation. Various Souvenir items, All-U-Can-Eat Buffets, Discounts in Gift Shops, etc. are included in certain venues. Modes of Transportation include Deluxe Motor Coach, Party Buses, various styles of Limousines, or Air Taxi if you have a small group!! Multiple pick up and drop off locations make traveling to the event a lot easier and much more enjoyable. Departure and Destinations include most major cities in the Midwest, Southeast, Northeast and Southwest – with more expansion to come!!!

www.thestadiumevents.com

THE STADIUM EVENTS LLC is proud to donate 10% of all profits from the sale of all Sports Card Checklists to a variety of well established National Charitable Organizations, as well as, Detroit area organizations. Track the amount dispersed to each organization on the website at www.thestadiumevents.com.

"Proceeds go to the fight against Breast Cancer"

To advertise in THE STADIUM EVENTS **Sports Card Checklist** call 586-879-6862 or e-mail quotes@thestadiumevents.com.

Advertising pricing is good for one year.

B & W advertising pricing:

Full Page......................$750

2/3 Page.......................$575

1/2 Page...................... $375

1/3 Page.......................$200

Business Card................$75

www.thestadiumevents.com

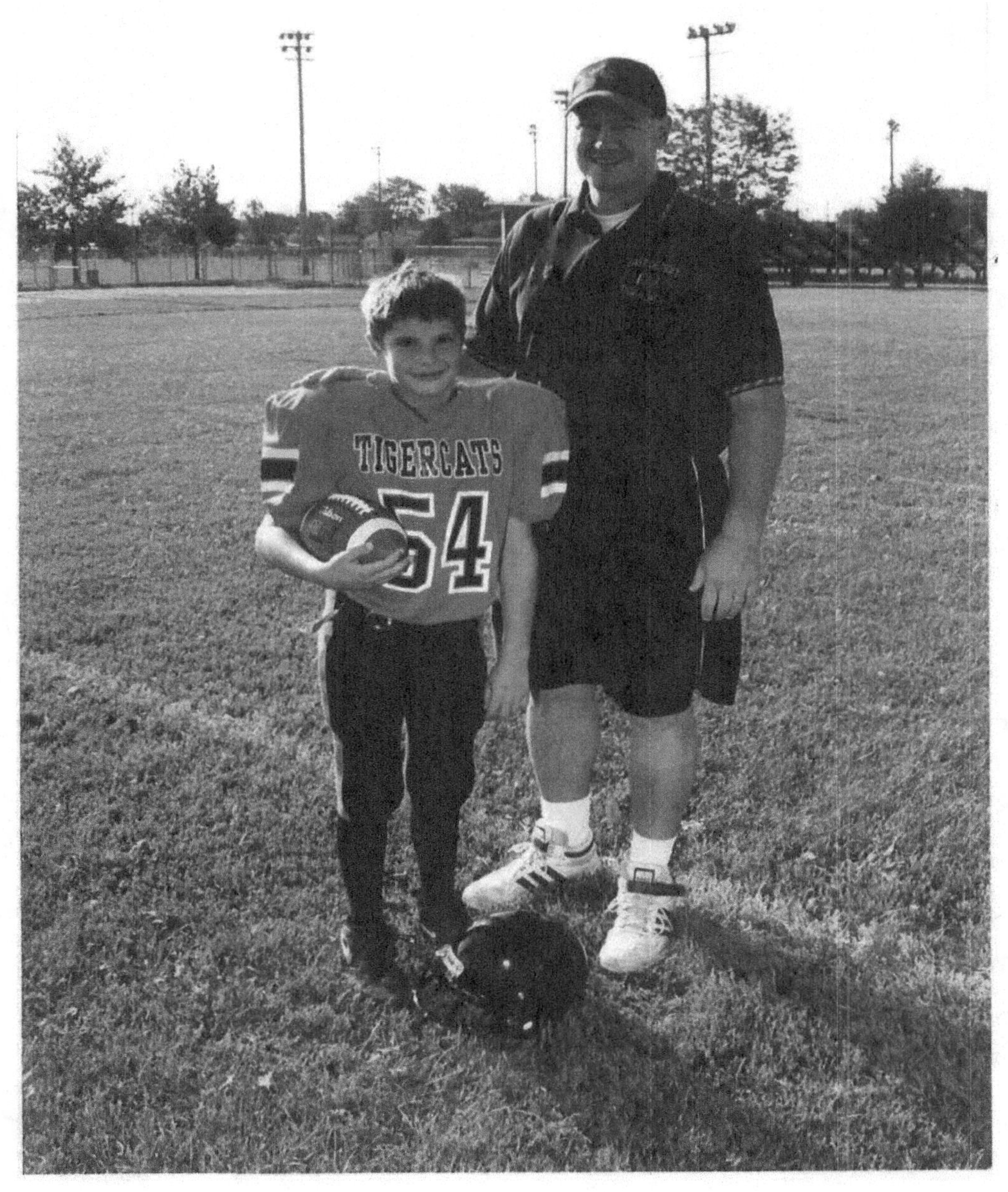

The Author / Owner of the Stadium Events Todd Hutson with son Zack during the 2003 Football Season with the East Detroit Tigercats. This was the last season of coaching Zack in Football and ended a great 4 year run of coaching with the Tigercats Organization. It was the most enjoyable and rewarding time I have had coaching youth sports.

You will notice Zack's football card from the 2003 season included on the Front Cover. That's because he happens to be **my** favorite football player of all time!!!

The Author / Owner of the Sportsmanship Vents Todd Hutton with son Zack during the 2003 Football Season with the East Detroit Titans. This was the last season of coaching Zack in football and ended a great seven years of coaching with the Titans organization. It was the most enjoyable and rewarding time I have had coaching youth sports.

You will notice Zack's football card from the 2003 season included on the Front Cover. That's because he happens to be my favorite football player of all time!!

Printed in the United States
By Bookmasters